People Are Living There

A DRAMA IN TWO ACTS

by Athol Fugard

SAMUEL FRENCH, INC.

25 WEST 45TH STREET   NEW YORK 10036
7623 SUNSET BOULEVARD   HOLLYWOOD 90046
LONDON   TORONTO

CHARACTERS

MILLY, *a Johannesburg landlady*
DON, *one of her lodgers*
SHORTY, *another of her lodgers*
SISSY, *Shorty's wife*

The first public performance of this play was given at the Hofmeyr Theatre Cape Town on June 14, 1969 with the following cast:

MILLY .... *Yvonne Bryceland*
DON .... *Athol Fugard*
SHORTY .... *Len Leach*
SISSY .... *Gillian Garlick*

The three main characters in this penetrating psychological study of frustration and loneliness spend an evening together in the kitchen of the cheap Johannesburg boarding house where they live.

There is Milly, the kindhearted slovenly landlady; Don, a cynical student layabout engaged in a permanent attempt to find himself and analyze others; and Shorty, a dim-witted postman, whose passions in life are boxing and silkworms. It is Milly's fiftieth birthday and, just jilted by the German lodger with whom she has lived for the past ten years, she asks the other two to join her in a wild birthday party—a gesture of defiance to prove to herself that she, too, is alive and can have a Good Time. The others rather reluctantly agree.

"*People Are Living There* confirms Fugard's position as perhaps the most important writer in the country today and ensures for him a place of honour in the history of South African theatre."

The Cape Times

3

People Are Living There

ACT ONE

*The kitchen of an old, double-storeyed house in
Braamfontein, Johannesburg. Two doors—one
leading to the backyard and an outside room
where* Don *lives, the other to a passageway and
so to the rest of the house. There is also a window
looking out onto a street. Center Stage is a kitchen
table and chairs with an electric light hanging
above them. For the rest we see, but not too
clearly because the light is bad, the walls, a
kitchen dresser, shelves and in one corner an old-
fashioned gas stove.*

*Curtain-up—early on a cold winter's evening. The
room is in darkness except for a little light from
the street outside. It is a Saturday night but still
too early for the rush of traffic to the city. Only
occasionally does the window catch the movement
of light as a car drives by. A figure appears in the
passage doorway. All we can see is the white blur
of a dressing gown. The figure stands motionless,
obviously listening, then calls out in a husky
woman's voice:*

Woman's Voice. "Hullo! Anybody home? (*Pause.*)
Help!"

(*Silence. A sudden, determined move to the door leading to the back-yard. Halfway across the room
this is stopped by the frail, silken chimes of a*

5

*grandfather clock somewhere else in the house.
The woman stops and listens. We hear the four
sets of chimes preceding the hour, then silence.
The woman turns and exits back into the passage
from which comes the sound of a blow to the
grandfather clock which now starts its belated
chiming of the hour. At the fourth stroke the
woman is back in the doorway. Three more. It is
seven o'clock. An arm comes up. The light goes on.
We see* MILLY. *About fifty years old, dressed in an
old candlewick dressing gown, her hair disordered,
her face swollen with sleep. She waits expectantly,
as if the light and chimes might evoke some
response in the silent house.*)

MILLY. Shorty! (*Silence. She directs her attention
very obviously to the ceiling and listens. Satisfied that
there is no sound of life,* MILLY *moves to the backdoor
and opens it, shivering and clutching her gown against
the cold night air.*) Hey Don. (*Louder.*) Don! (*She
waves.*) Jeez, it's cold hey!

VOICE. I'm busy.

MILLY. Winter all right. What are you doing?

VOICE. Leave me alone? (*Pause.* MILLY *shivers.*)

MILLY. Come on over and have some coffee. Warm
you up. That room of yours must be like a morgue.

VOICE. No. Go away.

MILLY. Suit yourself. Kettle's on all the same. (*She
closes the door with pretended indifference, then bends
down and peeps through the keyhole. Satisfied with
what she sees, she straightens up and goes around the
kitchen, looking for a cigarette, picking up and dis-
carding several empty packets before she finds the
right one. She lights a cigarette and waits, watching
the backdoor.* DON *comes in and moves straight for
the passage.*)

DON. Coming! (*Exit.* MOLLY *goes on smoking. Lavatory flushes off—in the passage.* DON *returns. Plain,
almost featureless face with a sallow complexion. Body*

*and movements without virility. He is about twenty
years old and is wearing a nondescript grey suit,
vaguely ill-fitting. Soft collared shirt, no tie. He stands
in the doorway frowning darkly at* MILLY.) What did
it look like to you?

MILLY. What?

DON. Me.

MILLY. Bladder-bursting.

DON. No no. In my room. What did you see?

MILLY. You, on your bed, on your back, looking up
at the ceiling.

DON. Nothing out of the ordinary?

MILLY. Hardly call that out of the ordinary.

DON. Purpose was dead in me. When I lay down at
four o'clock there were a hundred reasons why I should
have got up. When you saw me not one was left. I had
systematically abandoned the lot. Sartre calls it
Anguish.

MILLY. Still looking for it are you?

DON. I've told you before the expression is "finding
oneself."

MILLY. What's the difference?

DON. Nothing's lost in the way you make it sound.

MILLY. Well, according to the language I speak,
when I want to find something I'm looking for it, and
when I'm doing that I can be bloody certain I lost it
to begin with.

DON. Well, I never had it to begin with, so I can't
lose it.

MILLY. Good Lord!

DON. Look, this is beyond you.

MILLY. You're in trouble, my boy.

DON. Let's talk about something else please.

MILLY. What's all this got to do with Bachelor of
Commerce anyway? (DON *tries to ignore her.*) Because quite frankly it doesn't sound like studying to
me. For the sake of your poor parents I hope you are
going to pass this time.

DON. It's my life.

MILLY. And their money.

DON. In any case I've decided to chuck it up.

MILLY. Just like that! What happened?

DON. Accountancy.

MILLY. Again. How many times does that make?

DON. Only two.

MILLY. I don't think you try hard enough.

DON. Why should I? What's bookkeeping got to do with the dilemma of our age? I need time. I've worked it out. Fifty pounds a month will keep body and soul together, leaving my mind free. The paper is full of jobs.

MILLY. That doesn't sound like a career to me.

DON. An Age of Crisis, and you talk about a career. You're as bad as my parents. You'll be on to pension funds next.

MILLY. Doesn't worry me what happens to you, my boy. As long as I get my rent the lot of you can go down the drain for all I care.

DON. Then it's settled. Where's that coffee?

MILLY. (*Yawning.*) I've just woken up. Where are the others?

DON. Shorty's at the gym.

MILLY. That's right. Saturday. I forgot. And him? (*She indicates the ceiling.*) You see him go out?

DON. No.

MILLY. All quiet on the Western Front. (*Another yawn.*) Hell, my heart is still asleep. Anyway, I'll think I'll pop out. What's on your programme for tonight?

DON. Nothing. And I want to keep it that way.

MILLY. Well, I want a change in scenery. Get dressed in a mo. Maybe a walk. Brisk walk. Bit of fresh air. You could do with some too. It's healthy. What about it?

DON. The air outside is not as fresh as you think.

MILLY. Better than the lot in here thank you very much. You're going all pimply again.

DON. I never said I was good-looking.

MILLY. Maybe you eat too many sweets.

DON. Maybe I do.

MILLY. Well, there's something sickly somewhere.

DON. It's none of your business.

MILLY. Thank you.

DON. That coffee.

MILLY. I feel like a bit of excitement tonight. Movies or something. Been in all day.

DON. Where's that coffee?

MILLY. Coming. (*She doesn't move.*)

DON. So is Christmas.

MILLY. (*Looking at the ceiling.*) You sure you didn't see him go out?

DON. Why should I lie to you?

MILLY. To spite me. (DON *smiles.*) Yes! Don't think I don't know. There's a spiteful streak in you sometimes. (*Returns her attention to the ceiling.*) There's no sound of life.

DON. Maybe he's dead.

MILLY. Like hell.

DON. It was meant to be a joke.

MILLY. And I'm not laughing because it's not possible. Must have made a run for it behind my back. He knew I was waiting. Kept to his room all day. Did you notice? Avoiding me. There's proof. Guilty conscience! And then as soon as I closed an eye—the getaway! (*Stubs out her cigarette viciously and lights another, an automatic gesture.*) I didn't mean to—close my eye, I mean. I was lying down in wait for him. You know, spring the surprise when he got to the door. But the last thing I remember is Sissy's radio going full blast. Blah-blah-blah! God! I hated it. Get up Mildred, I said, get up and go up and grab it and chuck the bloody thing out! Blah-blah-blah! I must have dropped off then, because the next thing I knew it was cold and dark and . . . I don't know. Empty! Waking up is a cold business in an empty house.

Specially old houses. Wherever you look it's just walls.
God, it's depressing! Put out the light and you're as
good as in your grave. (DON *takes out a pencil and
makes a note on the back of one of the empty cigarette
packets.* MILLY *watches him.*) What did I say?

DON. That bit about the walls. The featureless face
of horror.

MILLY. I've got some pictures somewhere. We'll get
them up. (*Breaking mood.*) Anyway . . .

DON. Where's that coffee?

MILLY. Give me a chance to get my bearings!

DON. (*Looking at the stove.*) Isn't it on yet?

MILLY. I'll put it on in a minute.

DON. You told me the kettle was on.

MILLY. I did not.

DON. Milly you distinctly said "Kettle's on."

MILLY. Oh you're a liar!

DON. (*Putting away his pencil.*) In that case . . .

MILLY. Give it a rest man. You won't find youself
tonight.

DON. I came because you said the coffee was ready.

MILLY. Well I'm going to put the kettle on right
now. (*She stands.*)

DON. Call me when it's ready.

MILLY. (*Stopping his move to get up.*) Ssssssh! Activity! (*Goes quickly to the door, where she listens.*)
It's him! Must have been in the bathroom. So! Togging
himself up. Ever known him to have a bath on a Saturday? It's to spite me. God, I wish I knew where he was
going! (*She follows his movements in the room over-
head.*) Bed. Wardrobe. Dressing table. Putting on his
hair oil. Ever seen that? If you want to lose your
breakfast one morning go up and have a look. It's
enough to make any decent person sick. He sort of
washes those big paws of his in the stuff, smoothes
down the few hairs left on his nut and then smiles at
the result. It's revolting. Greenish. Looks like pepper-
mint liqueur.

DON. (*Standing.*) If you decide to make that coffee, call me.

MILLY. I'm putting it on now—*now*—right this very minute. Satisfied? (*She goes to the stove.*)

DON. Good. I'll be waiting.

MILLY. Sit down.

DON. Later.

MILLY. Sit down! I want to tell you something.

DON. I've heard enough.

MILLY. You don't know what I'm going to say so please sit down.

DON. You've got one minute. Well?

MILLY. (*Looking at the ceiling.*) Him.

DON. I knew it!

MILLY. Do you know what he's done?

DON. (*Emphatically.*) Yes!

MILLY. After ten years mark you. Ten years!

DON. I know.

MILLY. That's a good piece of anyone's life. Well? Isn't it?

DON. It is.

MILLY. You bet it is. Give me back those ten years and he'd never get the smell of them again. (*Pause.*) I'm not finished! (*Pause.*) It was a custom, Don. Every Saturday night. Regular as rent. Beer and sausages for two down at the Phoenix. Until tonight.

DON. Are you finished now?

MILLY. Yes. *No!* Wait. I just want to ask you one question. Is it right? Come on. Answer that. Smearing on his stinking hair oil. Is it right?

DON. It isn't.

MILLY. Then go up and tell him. You call yourself a man, don't you? Go up there and tell him it isn't right. And then hit him. A lady's honour is at stake. Ten years of her life. Hit him for it. (*With intensity.*) All that talk about meeting an old friend from Germany! Old friend, my foot. Where does *he* suddenly come from after ten years and a World War? And last week that new suit. For an old friend? From Germany? I wasn't born yesterday. I can also put one and one together and get two evil-minded birds in the bush.

(SHORTY LANGEVELD *appears in the passage doorway. He is short but stockily built, about twenty-five years old. He is wearing the tunic and trousers of a postman's uniform and carries a small bag and a pair of boxing gloves.*)

SHORTY. Hey, Milly.

MILLY. Go to hell, I'm busy.

DON. (*To* MILLY.) Go on.

MILLY. (*Realizing she has gone too far.*) Oh! So now you're interested.

DON. Two birds in the bush.

MILLY. I'll tell you some other time.

DON. Why not now?

MILLY. This is not the right moment.

SHORTY. Hey, chaps. Is Sissy gone?

MILLY. I'm not your wife's nursemaid. Damned good idea to get her one. For both of you. Kids. Man and Wife! (*To* DON.) You ever heard such nonsense?

SHORTY. Why you in such a bad mood, Milly?

MILLY. (*Shaking a finger at him.*) Don't you get impertinent with me, Shorty Langeveld! And take your togs out of here. I've told you before the kitchen's not a boxing ring. (*Exit* SHORTY *with bag and gloves.*) Gutless little whiner. He gets on my nerves. (DON, *who has been worrying* MILLY *with his intent stare, now laughs at her obvious discomfort.*) What's so funny?

DON. I'll tell you some other time.

MILLY. Don't bother. (MILLY *lights another cigarette.* SHORTY *returns.*)

SHORTY. What about some coffee to warm us up, Mill?

MILLY. Drop dead! (*She moves to the door.*)

SHORTY. (*In a whisper.*) What's wrong with her?

MILLY. (*At the door.*) I heard that.

DON. How did the boxing go?

SHORTY. We was sparring today. Major Jeffries says my defence is weak, but I got a sledge-hammer left, if I try. He's going to pick a team to fight Railways and Harbours in Durban at Christmas.

DON. Think you'll make it?

SHORTY. Well, Don, I'll try my best. Only this afternoon a guy called Jacobs rocked me, man. One-two, one-two then Dwada! Straight left, straight through. If it was for real, I would be out for the count.

DON. Use that left next time.

SHORTY. Sledge-hammer he says. If only I could get me a native for sparring partner it would be better. Specially Zulus. They is tough man! You can't just knock them out, you know. Their heads are hard. That's what Toweel does, I asked Emily if she's got any brothers and she said she will look. What about it sometimes, Don? Me and you. A few rounds.

DON. I'm a wrestler.

SHORTY. Judo-jitsu.

DON. Hari-kari, the lot.

SHORTY. You're bluffing! What you doing tonight?

DON. Nothing.

SHORTY. Same here. You seen Sissy! (*Takes out his paypacket.*) Payday!

DON. You're in the money!

SHORTY. (*Laughing.*) Ja! There's a guy at work—George—in the Despatch Room. He says: Paydays is happydays! We laught at him Don. He's always full of sports. But I got worries tonight. One pound ten from ten pound nineteen and six is nine pounds nine and six, right?

MILLY. (*Joining them at the table.*) And one week's bed and breakfast is four pound ten, please, plus six bob for washing.

SHORTY. Five bob.

MILLY. Six bob. There's a shilling fine. Emily says your socks were very smelly this week.

SHORTY. It's the walking, Milly. I sweat.

MILLY. Six bob!

SHORTY. (*Handing her the money.*) There's change.

MILLY. Are you accusing me of something?

VOICE. (*Suddenly and just beyond the passage doorway.*) Shorty!

SHORTY. Sissy!

VOICE. Shorty!

SHORTY. I'm in here Sissy.

VOICE. Well, I'm waiting.

SHORTY. I'm coming. (*To* DON.) Here goes. Hold your thumbs for me man. (*Hurries off.*) It was the trams, Siss. I waited . . .

VOICE. You said you would be home by seven. Where's the money? (MILLY *lays out two cups and saucers. Into each cup a teaspoon of instant coffee. Then condensed milk from a tin with two holes.*)

MILLY. She's a little bitch, that one. And he's a little fool.

DON. I have a feeling he knows.

MILLY. That makes it even more disgraceful. He should be ashamed.

DON. But he is.

MILLY. Then why doesn't he do something about it?

DON. Such as?

MILLY. I think that's perfectly obvious. To begin with, he could hit her.

DON. Violence won't solve his problem.

MILLY. Exactly. He's got no guts.

DON. Now there's a word I hate. What's guts?

MILLY. Guts? If you don't know what guts is, my boy, then I feel sorry for you. (*She adds hot water and sugar to the cups and sits down.*) "He's got guts." Let's see. (*Pause.*)

"Then up he rose
  With an awful sound

And smote the bastard down."
(*Chuckles with deep satisfaction.*) God that's good!
And smote the bastard down! Anyway, there you have
it. That's guts. If you can't hit out once in a while,
you might as well throw in the towel. (Don *has in the
meantime taken out a pipe—new—and is trying to
smoke it. Voices of* Sissy *and* Shorty *Offstage.*)

Shorty. Sissy . . .

Sissy. No.

Shorty. But . . .

Sissy. No!

Shorty. Please Sissy.

Sissy. (*Entering.*) I said *No!* (*White-faced, about
eighteen years old with straight, mouse-coloured hair.
Dressed with cheap extravagance. She is barefoot,
carrying her shoes and handbag.*) I'm sick of you and
those silkworms! Anyway you told me you threw
them away.

Shorty. (*Now also in the room.*) I did Sissy. Those
what you did prick and died.

Sissy. Oh! Hiding the others are you? From who?
From me? That's not very nice is it? They're mine
you know. Jossie gave them to me.

Shorty. You didn't want them. You never fed them.

Sissy. I want them now. Where are they? (*Pause.*)
Shorty Langeveld where are my silkworms? (*He
doesn't move.*) You know what you are? A bad boy.

Shorty. If you bring some beetroot leaves for them
to eat, I'll . . .

Sissy. (*Stamping her foot.*) I said N—O spells No!
Beetroot leaves! Ask some old Coolie shop for beetroot
leaves? On a Saturday night? Are you mad?

Shorty. (*Holding out a brown paper bag.*) Only a
few, Siss. If you put them in here nobody will see.

Sissy. And what will that make me look like? Going
to the movies with a brown paper bag! Full of beetroot
leaves. What will Billy think? "Beetroot leaves, Billy.
For Shorty." Yes. That's what I will say. "Shorty eats

beetroot leaves, Billy." He'll laugh at you, you know. He'll tell me again I'm married to a poep.

SHORTY. (*Prepared to suffer this.*) Okay.

SISSY. Ag! Why do I talk to you? (SISSY *turns away in disgust and goes to the stove where she collects a pair of stockings that have been hanging up to dry.* MILLY *and* DON *are drinking their coffee, watching the scene between the other two with detached interest.*)

MILLY. Since when is my stove your washing line?

SISSY. They got wet. I only got one pair. He's to blame. (*Pointing to* SHORTY.) Blame him. He's supposed to earn the living. (*Speaking to* SHORTY *again.*) Jossie's got five pairs you know. Five. And she hasn't even got a husband. (*On the point of putting on the stockings she turns to* SHORTY *who has been standing abashed, watching her.*) Where's your respect? Look the other way! (SHORTY *turns his back.*) What I would like to ask you, Shorty Langeveld, is what use is a husband that don't even bring home the living what he's supposed to earn?

SHORTY. (*His back turned.*) Please, Sissy.

SISSY. What sort of postman loses his letters! That's what I'd like to know.

SHORTY. Sissy!

SISSY. Ashamed of yourself, I hope. (*To* DON *and* MILLY.) I don't suppose he told you. One pound ten taken off because he lost letters again. It's not the first time. There he is. Ask him. You told Ma you could earn me a living. This is no married life. (*She is finished with her stockings.*) You can look now! (SISSY *puts on her shoes, then takes out lipstick, mirror, and powder-compact.*) You know what I warned you! Well, I mean it. Once more, oh boy! Just you come home once more with your pay short and I'll do it. I swear to God I'll do it. And it won't do you any good to cry.

SHORTY. Stop now, Siss!

SISSY. Yes, he cried. This big boy cried. Whaaa . . .

whaa . . . whaa. Real tears. "Don't, Sissy! Please Sissy! I promise, Sissy!" (SHORTY *has not yet turned to face her.*) I said you can look now. Turn around! (*He does so. The sight of him provokes her still more.*) Come here. Let's make you pretty.

SHORTY. (*Covering his mouth with his hands.*) No no.

SISSY. Tell Milly and Don what a pretty boy we make you in the room. Red lips, rosy cheeks. (*To* DON *and* MILLY.) He lets me do it upstairs. (*To* SHORTY.) Didn't you tell them? You don't seem to tell your friends anything about what goes on. You know what you are? (SISSY *leans forward suddenly and writes on his forehead with her lipstick.*) That's what you are! (*Picks up her bag and flounces out of the room.* SHORTY *stands hanging his head.* MILLY *and* DON *watch him.*)

MILLY. Shorty! Come here. (*He moves to* MILLY. *She examines his forehead.*) "Bad-boy." (DON *also examines it and then writes on the back of his cigarette packet.*) Why didn't you hit her? You're a boxer. Why didn't you give her one good wallop?

DON. Who's Billy?

MILLY. She says he's her cousin. Know what I mean?

DON. (*To* SHORTY.) You know him?

SHORTY. Sort of.

DON. Have you actually met him?

MILLY. Answer the man!

SHORTY. No.

MILLY. You idiot! Go on. Go and wash your face. (*Exit* SHORTY.) Satisfied? If that wasn't taking it lying down then I'd like to know what is. And let me assure you that's the only lying down she lets him do when she's around. You heard him. When a woman is stingy that way then she's really stingy. Dammit all, old Shorty's entitled to it.

DON. (*Looking up from his notes.*) The aggressive female and the submissive male. The loss of male virility and the woman's rebellion. The neurosis of our time.

MILLY. Who?

DON. Shorty and Sissy.

MILLY. (*Amazed.*) When?

DON. Now. Right here under our nose.

MILLY. This tiff? Come off it.

DON. Undercurrents, Milly. Undercurrents. Didn't you feel them. This room was like a dynamo. I couldn't have taken it much longer.

MILLY. What was going on? In plain language, please.

DON. She was trying to arouse Shorty.

MILLY. Nonsense. It's Billy she's after. I've seen it happen before. Shorty's just too dumb to see it.

DON. He knows all about it.

MILLY. Then why doesn't he do something?

DON. Because the thought of Billy and Sissy arouses him.

MILLY. Where in God's name do you get this rubbish from? Honestly, sometimes you can talk the biggest lot of . . .

DON. I'm not finished. There's something else. She knew I was watching. She was trying to arouse me as well.

MILLY. You sure?

DON. I should know.

MILLY. She's a little bitch, all right.

DON. I wanted to hit her.

MILLY. And where it hurts, I hope.

DON. She aroused a tremendous urge in me to grap hold of her and hit her. The way she put on her stockings? Did you catch that? I saw the suspenders you know. I think that was deliberate.

MILLY. I seem to have missed a hell of a lot.

DON. There's material here. (*Turns back to his notes.* SHORTY *returns, his face washed, carrying a large pair of black shoes. From a shelf at the back he collects a box containing polish, brush, etc., then settles down on a chair to clean the shoes.*)

MILLY. (*To* DON.) Work it out and let me know. There's obviously something going on and I don't know if I like it. I warn you, any high jinks and the lot of you get notice. I won't have it under my roof. (*She stares idly at* SHORTY.)

SHORTY. Spit and polish! Army style.

MILLY. (*With sudden suspicion.*) Let me see those? (SHORTY *hands her the shoes.*) Twelves!

SHORTY. Mr. Ahlers. He wants to see his face in them.

MILLY. You're helping him?

SHORTY. (*Still unsuspecting.*) He's going out so he asked me to do him a little favour and give his shoes a good shine. He's wearing his new suit.

MILLY. And you're going to? Help my worst enemy?

SHORTY. It's only a little favour.

MILLY. So whose side are you on?

SHORTY. Yours.

MILLY. Sneaking away behind my back to do *him* a little favour! That makes you the enemy.

SHORTY. I didn't know there was anything wrong.

MILLY. The impudence! To sit in front of me, in *my* kitchen, and clean *his* shoes. And think you can get away with it! Wait my boy. Zero hour is on its way . . . with no holds barred. (MILLY *leaves the table indignantly, but remains in the room.*)

SHORTY. (*To* DON.) You think I should polish?

DON. Go ahead. Don't let her bully you.

SHORTY. (*Polishing.*) It's hell tonight, hey! And I'm trying to say the right things. You know Don . . . Girls? I give up. What do they want? You try your best but they is still unhappy. Like Sissy. She's unhappy, I know. But what must I do? There's always struggles in life, isn't that so? I tell her. Sissy, I say, there's always struggles in life.

DON. What does she say?

SHORTY. "Well struggle harder!" Hey? And I sweat, Don. On my rounds. And at Christmas, when it's three rounds and also parcels. Boy, then I sweat! You know what I think it is. Love takes a long time for a woman. You just got to keep your trap shut and wait.

MILLY. (*Moving to* SHORTY *at the table.*) Does he look frightened? Ahlers?

SHORTY. No.

MILLY. Well he'd better be. And when you take back those shoes you can tell him I said so. Before he leaves this house tonight, I want a straight answer to a few simple questions.

SHORTY. I'll tell him, Milly. (*She moves away again.*)

DON. How long have you been married?

SHORTY. Going on for six months. I met her down by Booysens. Her Ma's place. Forty-nine Vereeniging Road. I was still a telegram boy then. Her Oupa died you see. So I gave her Ma the telegram and when she reads it she cries, Don! Hell, man, that old woman cries there on the back stoep. Sissy was in the yard. They got an old tyre hanging from a tree there . . . for a swing, you know. She was swinging. Anyway, her Ma was crying there and Sissy calls out: "What's wrong Ma?" So I take off my cap and I go over and tell her. She asked my name. That's how we got friends with each other. (*He is polishing the shoes all the time.*) We went like that for maybe six months. Then I reckoned we were ready. I spoke to Sissy and she said it was okay. She wanted to get married for a change. Her Ma asked me if I was making enough money and I said yes. So she said it was certainly okay by her and may God help me. (*Pause . . . he puts down the shoes.*) But there's one thing Don. We wasn't married in a Church. It was by Special Licence. She was in a hurry, you see. The man in charge said it was okay and we could now go ahead. Because it's legal, you see. I got the certificate. But it was so quick!

Just like seeing somebody for a job. You put on your suit, you get your papers, and your Ma and your Pa, and the Bride-to-be. Then there's some questions and more papers . . . and then you got it, you think. But when we got home—we had our honeymoon in the Shamley Boarding House in De Korte Street—well, when we got there, we wasn't so sure we got it. That's the trouble, Don. I think Sissy is still not so sure we got it. She gets scared.

Don. How long do you give yourself?

Shorty. What?

Don. Your marriage. How long do you think it will last?

Shorty. Forever.

Don. In the face of all this . . . ! (*Turns to his notes.*)

Shorty. We do love each other.

Don. Let's discuss this objectively. What do you think love means?

Shorty. Well, I say to love something is to like it a lot, and more than anything else. And you?

Don. Suppose I say sex.

Shorty. You mean . . . ?

Don. Yes. I put it to you that the heart of love throbs below the belt. Very good! (*Makes a note.*) Yes?

Shorty. (*Strongly.*) No!

Milly. (*Back at the table.*) For one thing there's that little matter of the fifty pounds which he's so conveniently forgotten about. Well, I haven't. And if he walks through that door tonight I want it back, cash, plus ten years' interest. You can tell him that, too. Did he say where he was going?

Shorty. No.

Milly. Don't just say no! Think.

Shorty. He just said he was going out. (Milly *resumes her pacing. To* Don.) I would love Sissy even if she only had one leg and eye!

DON. You sure? Picture it.

SHORTY. Yes! Shame, Don!

DON. Aha! Pity. That's something else. It's no good, Shorty, there's only one way out. The womb! A man called Freud discovered it. Do you dream?

SHORTY. Yes.

DON. Give me one.

SHORTY. Well, these days I'm in this building with this letter to deliver. And its registered, which makes it worse. My bag is weighing like lead. Hell, it's heavy man! But there's hundreds of postboxes and I can't find the right one and somebody is shouting: "Hurry up, man! It's urgent!" And I'm looking and sweating and that bag is heavy and then I wake up.

DON. Do you ever find the right box?

SHORTY. No.

DON. Who's the letter addressed to?

SHORTY. I'll look next time.

DON. It's as clear as daylight. The registered letter is phallic, the boxes are female, the bag is your conscience. That's why it's heavy. Mark my words, one night you'll open it and find Sissy inside. (*A thoughtful* MILLY *is again at the table.*)

MILLY. Shorty. Do you want to wipe out the past with a favour?

SHORTY. Anything, Mill.

MILLY. I want you to do something for me when you take back those shoes. So make them shine! We'll use them as bait. I think I've got it, Don. (*To* SHORTY.) But you must be careful.

SHORTY. (*Polishing industriously.*) Okay.

MILLY. Very careful!

SHORTY. (*Uneasy.*) What is it?

MILLY. Shorty, my darling, it's a trap.

SHORTY. (*Now nervous.*) I don't know if I can do that.

MILLY. Of course you can. Polish! I've definitely got it Don! Now we'll see who gets the last laugh. (*To*

SHORTY.) Now listen. You're going to take back those shoes. Right?

SHORTY. Right.

MILLY. When you give them back start talking.

SHORTY. About what?

MILLY. Anything. You were talking to him about something this morning.

SHORTY. Mario Lanza.

MILLY. So talk about him again, or the shoes, or anything—just get him talking. Then you ask casually: "Where are you going Mr. Ahlers?" You got that?

SHORTY. Yes.

MILLY. Casually you understand. Get his answer, then high-tail it back here. (SHORTY *hesitates.*) You said you would do me a favour. Anything. Didn't he say anything, Don?

DON. He did.

MILLY. Thank you. Well?

SHORTY. Start talking.

MILLY. Casually.

SHORTY. Where are you going, Mr. Ahlers?

MILLY. But for God's sake causally or else he'll smell a rat. Well go on! (*Exit a worried* SHORTY.) We've got him, Don. He've got him. Stand by for action.

DON. I haven't volunteered.

MILLY. You'd better, before all hell breaks loose.

DON. I'll stay neutral. Every fight needs a ref.

MILLY. Not this one. It's going to be foul. There's a month's free bed and breakfast in it for you.

DON. What do I have to do?

MILLY. The plan is as follows. Shorty tells us where he is going. Our first move is to get dressed. We tog up to kill the cats. My white costume with matching gloves! You'll see something tonight my boy. That done we then descend on the enemy. Ha! That will be triumph. He's sitting there you see, with his so-called friend from Germany, and in we march, sit

down and have a good time of our own! And right
under his nose where he can see us. Then when he
comes crawling to ask if he can join in, I'll have him
arrested for molesting. (SHORTY *appears timidly in the
doorway.*)

SHORTY. Milly . . .

MILLY. (*Eagerly.*) Well?

SHORTY. I tried, but he just said thank you and
closed the door.

MILLY. (*Hissing.*) Then go back there and knock!

SHORTY. (*Hissing back.*) You didn't say nothing
about knock Milly. Hey, Don? You just said . . .

MILLY. Then listen. Knock! Say you want to borrow
a razor blade or something, then Mario Lanza, then
where are you going, Mr. Ahlers? But casually!

SHORTY. Where are you going . . . (*Exit.*)

MILLY. (*With a premonition of disaster.*) I'll mur-
der that little runt if he makes a mess of this.

DON. Suppose it's that place he goes to sometimes
. . . the German Club. You've got to be a member.

MILLY. We'll gatecrash. And if they chuck us out,
then we'll do it on the pavement outside.

DON. What?

MILLY. Laugh and sing and be happy. So will you.
Yes! You're coming! You'll tell me jokes and make
me laugh, loudly, so that he can hear.

DON. I've never faced a prospect like this in all my
life.

MILLY. You'll survive. It's him I'm after. (SHORTY
is back in the doorway, obviously frightened of MILLY.
*He moves so as to keep the kitchen table between
them.*)

SHORTY. I did like you said, Milly.

MILLY. And?

SHORTY. (*Faltering.*) And . . . Mr. Ahlers . . . he
said . . .

DON. Thank God!

MILLY. Go on.

SHORTY. . . . to tell you that he knows I don't shave and . . .

MILLY. Yes?

SHORTY. . . . and that he is going out to dinner with an old friend from Germany.

MILLY. (*Quietly.*) Come here, Shorty.

SHORTY. No.

MILLY. Will you kindly come here.

SHORTY. I did it just the way you said, Milly.

MILLY. (*Now impotent with anger.*) Shorty Langeveld come here this very minute.

SHORTY. What are you going to do?

MILLY. I don't know yet . . .

SHORTY. I'll ask him again.

MILLY. (*Stops and listens.*) Ssssssh! (*Moving to the door.*) It's him! (*To* SHORTY.) Sit down! (*She lights a cigarette.*) Sit down, I said.

SHORTY. You're not cross with me no more?

MILLY. Sit down. Talk to Don. Pretend nothing's happened. It's him all right. (*She goes to the door and takes up a pose of studied indifference, her arms folded, smoking. In a loud voice, and heavily sarcastic to start with.*) As I was saying chaps fine feathers making fine birds is one thing but a bald head that can't even speak the English language properly, is another. There's not a hope in hell for you know who, even in a new suit. So it's no good anybody trying to get classy ideas around here, because we know all about it! (*Now speaking directly to Ahlers, who is in the passage.*) Enjoy yourself . . . with your old friend from Germany. And please don't worry about me. I'll just sit here in the kitchen and twiddle my thumbs. After all it was only ten years. Why worry about them! (*Her anger and resentment beginning to break through.*) Well, you'd better, because they were mine. Those were ten years of my life and you had them cheap. Just don't think that means I'm hardup for you. Because I've got a surprise for you, Mr.

Big Shot. I'm also going to have a good time tonight. You bet. I'm going to have the best good time
of my life. And it won't be beer and sausages at the
Phoenix! Put that where the monkey puts his nuts.
And when you come home I'll be out and there'll be
an account for fifty pounds in your bed. (*Now shouting and gradually moving out of sight into the passage.*) Because if you think this is the end of me
you've got another guess coming. I've only started.
(*Front door slams.*) Yes go on! Go on, get the hell
out of here, you rotten stinking thief. *Thief!* (*Silence.
The clock chimes, then one stroke. The sound of a
vicious blow. The clock strikes seven more times. It is
eight o'clock. The window reflects heavy traffic in the
street outside.* SHORTY *and* DON *wait.* MILLY *appears
quietly in the doorway, standing there for a few
seconds before moving to the table for a cigarette.*)
You heard that, I hope? (SHORTY *and* DON *nod.*)
Good! I'm glad. I wanted to humiliate him in public,
and I think I succeeded. You should have seen him.
He crawled through that door like a dog with his tail
between his legs. (*Pause. With an edge of suspicion.*)
What did you hear?
  SHORTY. You told him Milly.
  MILLY. Where to get off! Didn't I?
  SHORTY. To get out!
  DON. And go to hell.
  MILLY. Thank you. Enough! Let's leave it at that.
Because I meant it. Every solitary syllable. I *am* going
out and I *am* going to have a good time. Because, just
between you and me, the old Phoenix was a bit of
a flop the last couple of times. Strictly speaking that
makes this a stroke of luck. A chance to really enjoy
myself for a change. In fact why not the three of us.
There's an idea! Let's make it a trio.
  SHORTY. What Mill?
  MILLY. Anything. You're invited.
  SHORTY. I'm game.

MILLY. Settled. I'll get dressed. (*She sits.*) Where are we going?

DON. Nowhere.

MILLY. You promised.

DON. I did not.

MILLY. I'm ignoring you. (*To* SHORTY.) Your turn. Think. Give us a bright idea.

SHORTY. There's still time for the second session.

MILLY. The movies?

SHORTY. At the Roxy . . .

MILLY. Seen it.

SHORTY. What about the Plaza. They is showing . . .

MILLY. Seen that, too.

SHORTY. I'll get the paper.

MILLY. I've seen them all. The movies! Who the hell wants to go to the movies?

SHORTY. You said . . .

MILLY. I said think of a bright idea for a good time. Don't you understand the English language? A good time!

DON. The movies are all right, Mill.

MILLY. "The movies are all right, Mill." (*Turns to the window.*) Look out there. Go on, look! Thousands of them. Millions. Where are they going? They're going to have a good time. Every Saturday night they drive past on their way to have a good time. And don't try to tell me they're going to the movies! So what I want to know is, where is it? (SHORTY *smiles.*) Don't just sit there grinning like an ape. Go out and ask them. (SHORTY *laughs with embarrassment.*) What are you laughing at? Go out and ask them.

SHORTY. No Milly.

MILLY. Yes Milly! Go out there and stop one of those cars and say Milly wants to know where is it? Where do you get this good time every Saturday night? She's stuck in her kitchen with two good-for-nothing nitwits, so can she come?

DON. (*Tapping out his pipe.*) You're not going to

like this Milly but I feel I've got to tell you. Your good time is an illusion.

MILLY. Listen to him!

DON. It doesn't exist.

MILLY. You haven't even looked for it, so stop talking.

DON. Because I know I won't find it. It's not there. It's a hoax.

MILLY. Why don't you dry up! I've had them— Good times! And when I walk out of here now, in ten minutes' time, I'll find another.

DON. It's like the sandwiches I took to school. Polony or jam. In a toffee tin. Somebody else had the toffees.

MILLY. What the hell are you talking about now?

DON. Life with a capital F. There's no mystery, Milly. That's what you want to believe. Romance around every corner. Adventure at the bottom of the street. The classic lower—middle-class illusion. I'm telling you it's polony or jam. Will you believe it that in my twenty years I have never yet once been surprised?

MILLY. Well you had better start! Because it's not all like that. (*Indignant.*) There's a hell of a lot of mystery, my boy. Going on all the time. And surprises. Oh yes! I could tell you a thing or two that would surprise you.

DON. Impossible. What?

MILLY. Aha! About me for example. (DON *laughs.*) You think you know all the answers? Well, you don't. Because I could tell you something about me that would make your hair stand on edge. (SHORTY *is busy at a shelf behind* MILLY's *back.*)

DON. Go ahead.

MILLY. It happens to be a secret. (SHORTY *knocks over a pot.*) What are you doing there?

SHORTY. Nothing.

MILLY. Liar! Come here.

SHORTY. (*A shoebox in his hands.*) Just my silk-worms.

MILLY. (*In horror.*) And where have you been keeping them?

SHORTY. Sissy doesn't . . .

MILLY. Well neither do I!

SHORTY. Just that old pot what you never use, Mill.

MILLY. Suppose they escape and crawl into the food?

SHORTY. They was in our room Milly, but Sissy sticks pins in them. They don't do nothing. They are nearly all in the silk already.

MILLY. (*Vaguely interested.*) Let me see?

DON. Is it something you did?

MILLY. What?

DON. Your secret.

MILLY. I'm not telling.

DON. Something that was done to you?

MILLY. Try again. (SHORTY *puts the shoebox on the table in front of* MILLY.)

SHORTY. I was feeding them. Beetroot leaves.

MILLY. (*Examining the contents of the box.*) Well I'll be . . . ! Just look at that, will you. You seen this, Don?

SHORTY. They was just so small when Jossie gave them to me.

MILLY. Cosy, isn't it. Sort of a pod. Nature is damn marvellous when you come to think of it.

DON. Simple! An accident of birth. (MILLY *looks at him.*) Your secret.

MILLY. There were no accidents. I arrived on the dot, head first, six pounds four ounces with everything where it should be. They say I hardly cried.

DON. I mean something before birth. Like your father being the Prince of Wales.

MILLY. There's good blood. But I wouldn't go as far as that. Jenkins is an old Port Elizabeth name.

Don. Then there's nothing. There's no secret. You're just making it up.

Milly. (*With a superior smile.*) Suit yourself. I'm saying nothing. (Don *is still intrigued.* Milly *returns her attention to the silkworms.*) So this is silk. And to think worms do it! Do they . . . how do they do it?

Shorty. From the back.

Milly. Their bowels?

Shorty. Yes.

Milly. (*Highly indignant.*) No they don't! Don, where does the silk come from?

Don. Two glands in the head.

Milly. That's better. (*To* Shorty.) How could it be precious if you were right? (Don *now also examines the worms.*)

Milly. (*To* Shorty.) That's all. (Shorty *smiles.*) You can go now! (Shorty *moves to one side with his shoebox.*)

Don. Let's get back to your secret.

Milly. (*Delighted.*) Got you guessing have I? Thought you knew everything.

Don. Be honest with me, Milly. Is there definitely a secret?

Milly. (*Simply, convincingly.*) Yes, it's there all right. Something happened. I feel it, Don. Nowadays more and more. It gets so bad sometimes I don't want to look or listen anymore. Honestly. Because when I do . . . I don't know . . .

Don. Something sad.

Milly. Sort of.

Don. Pain.

Milly. It hurts.

Don. You cried.

Milly. I'll confess to a tear or two, on occasions.

Don. If I said Horror would that be going too far?

Milly. Horror? Maybe. Horrible? Could be.

Don. Horror, pain, sadness, and you were young.

Milly. Christ, what a life!

Don. I've got it! You were raped.

MILLY. (*Indignant.*) By whom?

DON. Wait! Let me give you the picture. I'm good at this. You were on your way to school, a sweet little girl in her gym slip and black stockings . . . Garters! . . . when you met this man who'd been hiding behind a tree. You're innocent, you see. So when he offered you toffees you ate one. Then came the suggestions. When you resisted, he forced you down . . .

MILLY. I'd like to see anyone try!

DON. It happens every day.

MILLY. Mind you, there was that old le Roux once, when me and Beryl Conwright were on the swings. But hell! You could hardly call that rape. No! Try again.

DON. What about your mother? She was raped and you're the result.

MILLY. Mommy! I'd have liked to see someone try something with her. She was as strong as an ox.

DON. There's still your father. Why do you never mention him?

MILLY. (*Promptly.*) Alfred Jenkins, storeman, grade one, on the South African Railways. Retired on pension. You won't find anything there.

DON. Not so fast, not so fast. Let's probe.

MILLY. Dig as deep as you like. Southend Cemetery, if you want to know. Him and Mommy. Side by side. There's an angel pointing upwards.

DON. Little girls and their daddies! Psychology's got a word for it.

MILLY. What are you getting at?

DON. The realm of the subconscious Milly. Where lusts and libidos writhe like tormented serpents.

MILLY. Good God!

DON. Yes! So let's have a look at Alfred. Did he drink?

MILLY. Daddy had his pots on a Saturday night with the other exservicemen.

DON. That's enough. Too much is anaesthetic. Too little leaves the inhibitions intact.

MILLY. Hurry up! I haven't got all night.

DON. Here's the picture. It's a Saturday night. The pubs have closed. You're in your room, in bed . . . in the dark! Your mother is asleep. She's the ailing sort—psychosomatic. The front door opens and closes. Silence. You think: that must be Daddy. You lie and listen. The footsteps hesitate then lurch towards *your* room. The door opens, the door closes, and you know he's in the room. You can hear him breathing heavily. Daddy, you say. Silence. Then a few more steps. He's at your bed now. You can smell brandy fumes . . .

MILLY. Stop! (DON *laughs*.) It's disgusting.

DON. Watch it, Milly. Guilt!

MILLY. Alfred Jenkins was a good man. If he could hear what you've just said he'd turn in his grave. And Mommy, too.

DON. It's good enough for a Trauma.

MILLY. Well, you're wrong. You're on the wrong track altogether.

DON. Give me a clue.

MILLY. I'll tell you when you get hot. (*Lights a cigarette, now thoroughly absorbed in the game.*)

DON. Was it something sudden?

MILLY. Give me the picture.

DON. There you are, a young girl in a white dress, full of hope . . .

MILLY. You're getting warm.

DON. . . . life is peaceful. You are happy. Until suddenly, like a bolt from the blue, it happens. The dream is shattered and you are set on your hopeless journey through dark and dusty rooms. How's that?

MILLY. (*Emphatic.*) No! It wasn't like that at all.

DON. (*Still under the momentum of his thought.*) An early marriage!

MILLY. No.

DON. A death? A suicide?

MILLY. No.

DON. Then life. Birth! What about a baby?

MILLY. (*With sudden vehemence.*) *No!* There was

no baby. And I don't care, because I don't want babies. Understood? Finished. Settled. Next one.

DON. So then it took its time.

MILLY. Come again?

DON. Whatever happened to the young girl in the white dress, happened slowly.

MILLY. "It took its time." My time . . . bit by bit . . . yes! That sounds better. Slow, and sly. What I mean is I try to remember when. The Moment When— the way they say: "And from then on so and so" . . . and so on. But I can't. There doesn't seem to be a day or a date. Once upon a time it wasn't, now it is, but when or where . . . ? It's not easy to pin down. Believe me, I've tried.

DON. Milly, do *you* know what it is? (*She smokes.*) You mean you *don't* know?

MILLY. (*Irritably.*) Wouldn't be much of a secret if I knew would it!

DON. Just as I thought. You're making it up.

MILLY. I'm not.

DON. This secret is a figment of your imagination. In my opinion you're compensating for a colourless existence by inventing . . .

MILLY. Sometimes I could brain you! What do you know about it?

DON. Apparently as much as you. Nothing. Which most likely means there is nothing.

MILLY. Nothing! I said it hurts, didn't I? Can nothing hurt? I'll say it again, as God is my witness, it hurts. And it took its time. Mine. And once upon that time there was a little girl in a white dress, full of hope, and she was happy. But now she's not any more. Is that my imagination? Those are facts.

DON. But not scientific facts. I can't measure them. You tell me it hurts. But what can a scientist do with that. Unless you can be more specific give it up and suffer in silence.

MILLY. You mean the details?

DON. Call them what you like.

MILLY. (*Stalling*.) You're asking for the details.

DON. Yes.

MILLY. Okay.

DON. I'm waiting.

MILLY. Let's see . . . it hurts.

DON. Where?

MILLY. All over.

DON. I give up.

MILLY. Hold your horses. We'll try again. It's hurts. An ache. A sort of dull ache.

DON. Go on.

MILLY. Yes, it's coming now. It hurts. There's pain. Sometimes . . . sometimes it's in the colour of things. They go grey. Yes. I'm on to it! Things go grey. Know what I mean? Dull. Dreary. For days on end. And the days too. Sunday, Monday even Someday . . . all grey. Faces, and calendars and the right time when I look at the kitchen clock and then the taste of the next cigarette—all of them seem to lose their colour. It's enough to make me sick. If you're looking for symptoms, there's one. I get sick. In the afternoons, when I look at the clock and I see it's some old time again, I could vomit. And the way things can suddenly . . . (*Looking for words*.) . . . Be! You know, there It Is. Let's just say things get me down.

DON. Don't stop now!

MILLY. Well, I walk into a room—I'm by myself because he's at work and you're somewhere else and it's all quiet so I'm alone—then I walk into a room and I stand still and think about something to do. I look around, you see, for a little task to while away the time. And then it comes. I begin to notice. It's like a plug has been pulled out and something's drained away down a big, black hole, leaving everything stranded. Things stand too still. Chairs and tables. All empty and still . . . and stupid. That's the word! Stupid. Like that chair. I know what it is. I look at

it and I say Chair. But it doesn't help. It goes on being
empty and useless. Once it got so bad I said: Well
I'll prove it. So I sat down. But that made it even
worse.

DON. (*Eagerly.*) Because then *you* felt stupid!

MILLY. Exactly.

DON. You saw yourself—an object called Milly in
an object called chair—but knowing the names didn't
help because everything went on being useless, includ-
ing yourself.

MILLY. You've got it.

DON. (*Excited.*) For God's sake, Milly, that's Anguish!

MILLY. Let's move on.

DON. Wait! We've got a situation here. You're in
that chair and you think: Enough! Move! or Get Up!
. . . one of the commands. But nothing happens. You
think about it, but the reasons for moving break like
bad string when you try to pull out of your inertia . . .

MILLY. We've already had that!

DON. This is a development. Now you're conscious
of what is happening.

MILLY. Well, let's cut it short. I'm conscious. Now
I move.

DON. Right. You stand up.

MILLY. That's better. Erect! I walk again.

DON. Walking consists of picking up one foot, swinging it forward and putting it down. For a fraction of a
second you stand precariously on one leg. Then you
remember the other one so up it comes, and again forward and down. While this is going on there's the
problem of your arms at your sides, your heart is beat-
ing, your chest rising and falling with breathing, your
eyeballs swivelling in their sockets . . .

MILLY. Is it as bad as that?

DON. I have a dream. Music is playing, and I'm in
a corner and so far no one has seen me. I think it's a
party because there's a lot of people, and . . . well,

all I know about them really is the noise, because I'm not watching. I'm holding my breath. But the noise is a hubbub—talking and jokes and one very loud voice laughing heartily. Then the music stops. I can't tell you how terrible that is. Just stops. Silence. And sweat. Because I know, I just know that that means *it's my turn.* Don't ask me what. That's the thought. *It's your turn now!* I feel their eyes. Without looking up I know they are staring and waiting and that it is my turn and I must do something. So I move. I walk. One foot up, a second on one leg, then down. Two or three steps, in this silence, safely. Then things start to go wrong. I begin to wobble during that second on one leg, my arms start swinging wildly. There's a feeling that I've got five elbows and they're all sticking out. I'm knocking glasses into people's laps, falling over their legs . . .

MILLY. Wake up!

DON. I always do. The trouble is I wake up too soon. I never reach the end. The terror, you see. My mind protecting itself.

MILLY. It's only a dream. You said so yourself.

DON. But don't you also feel it? How can I put it? The fit. A feeling that things don't fit. Either life is sizes too big or you're too small. Something's wrong somewhere and maybe that is why people stare.

MILLY. At what?

DON. You haven't reached the stage where they stare?

MILLY. At what?

DON. You.

MILLY. No.

DON. It will come. A feeling of being watched, of people waiting, because it's *your* turn. Some pull it off of course. Others make a mess of it, like my dream, and have to leave the party. The failures. You've seen them, those old sticks of skin and bone sitting at the edge of oblivion on park benches. It's happened.

MILLY. Hold on.

DON. Decrepit, decaying . . .

MILLY. Wait!

DON. Neglecting themselves, neglected by others, forgotten . . .

MILLY. *What?*

DON. They've been forgotten. It happens long before you are dead.

MILLY. What do you mean, forgotten?

DON. You loose your place in the mind of man. With a bit of luck once or twice in your life you have it. That warm nest in another mind where "You" is all wrapped up in their thinking and feeling and worrying about "You." But even if you are one of the lucky ones, sooner or later you end up in the cold again. Nothing is forever. They die, or you get divorced. One way or another they go, they forget, and you end up in your little room with your old age pension and a blind bitch for friendship. From then on it's just a matter of days. When they're good, the two of you crawl out to a bench in the sun where she can hate the pigeons and you can hate the people. When it gets dark, you crawl back to the room. Until one day, one more sunny day with the pigeons flocking and the people passing, you're not there. But who misses you? Who's to know that inside a room, finally, forgotten by the world . . .

MILLY. Rubbish. That's absolute rubbish. Morbid muck.

DON. Read the papers. There are cases every day.

MILLY. For God's sake man! This is a civilized country. Nobody gets forgotten like that. One thing I can assure you, it's not happening to me. Oh no! There are limits. (*Pause.*) What were the cases!

DON. A few days ago. An old woman. They had to break down the door. She was found . . .

MILLY. I don't want to hear!

DON. Suit yourself. But it's happening . . .

MILLY. I said . . .

DON. Here! Tonight!

MILLY. Who?

DON. You. Him. Me. (*With sudden violence.*) Are you blind? It Happens! Who remembers us? At this moment? Ahlers? Is he thinking about you? With his old friend from Germany? (*Turning to* SHORTY, *who has been following the argument for several minutes.*) Or Sissy? Billy-boy has just made her laugh. She's enjoying herself. She's forgotten she's got a husband, who he is, where he is. And you're waiting. You are waiting for her to remember you, to come back. And when they do, when they walk in and find us again, it will be the way you find something old and forgotten and almost useless. Something in a corner, put away a long time ago, and now there it is again, too broken to mend but too much trouble to throw away. So back it goes, because maybe one day . . . That's us! We're hanging on by a maybe in somebody else's mind. (*Pause.*) I'm finished. (*He sits down and smokes his pipe.*)

SHORTY. (*To* MILLY.) What's going on?

MILLY. Shut up.

SHORTY. (*To* DON.) Sissy misses me. She does Don. She always comes home.

MILLY. I said shut up! (*Tries to light a cigarette.*) Is it my imagination or is it cold in here? My hands are like ice. (*Exit* SHORTY.) So who cares?

DON. That's another way of putting it. Who cares?

MILLY. I mean *me*—about *him*. Because it so happens I'm not hard-up, you see. You forgot about that. In fact I forget him sometimes. For hours on end. Pottering around in here, I forget him completely. The other day, playing patience, it was quite a surprise when he walked in because he was clean out of my mind. And tonight. If you think I'm going to spend my night thinking about him you've got another guess coming. I've got plans which will take my mind right off the subject. (SHORTY *returns with his pair of boxing gloves which he offers to* MILLY.) What's this?

SHORTY. You said your hands were cold.

MILLY. But boxing gloves!

SHORTY. They are warm.

MILLY. Oh well. Try anything once. But only for a second you understand. (*She is putting them on.*) I've got to get dressed in a mo. Sssssh!

(*Inside the house the clock begins to chime. They listen. The sixteen chimes end. The clock strikes three.*)

SHORTY. Three o'clock.

MILLY. Go and hit it. (*Exit* SHORTY. *A timid blow. Silence.*) I said hit it! Imagine it's Sissy. (*A second blow. The clock continues its striking.* MILLY *is obviously counting. After the sixth stroke she relaxes. But the clock strikes once more.*) Can't be.

DON. What?

MILLY. Ten o'clock. I counted nine and then it struck again.

DON. Then it's ten o'clock.

MILLY. No. Don.

DON. All right, so it's eleven.

MILLY. No, no! It's nine o'clock.

DON. Never.

MILLY. The last time that clock struck it was eight.

DON. We must have been talking and didn't hear it.

MILLY. Nonsense. Shorty!

DON. Why get so agitated. Nine, ten, eleven, twelve . . .

MILLY. Shorty!

DON. Yesterday, tomorrow . . .

MILLY. (*Violently.*) Shorty!

SHORTY. (*Offstage.*) I'm in here! (*Exit* MILLY *hurriedly into the passage.* DON *waits, smoking his pipe.* MILLY *returns slowly.*)

DON. Well? (MILLY *says nothing*.) It's ten o'clock. I told you. Two left. So much for today.

MILLY. What do you mean by that?

DON. It's ten o'clock, which, when you work it out, means that there are two hours left of today.

MILLY. (*In growing agitation*.) So do you think I can't add?

DON. Correction. It's a subtraction sum. A taking away. (*Watching* MILLY *closely*.) More and more. (*Pause*.) Until you've had the lot and then you're dead. Adding never comes into it.

MILLY. Well just remember, Mr. Donovan Big-brain, it's also happening to you.

DON. (*Tapping on the table with his pipe*.) The passing seconds. Stop them. (*He taps*.) Go on! The sound of doom, Milly. Seconds becoming minutes, minutes becoming hours, days, months, years . . .

MILLY. All right!

DON. You said ten, didn't you?

MILLY. What?

DON. Years. With Ahlers. That makes a total of three thousand six hundred and fifty-two days, allowing for leap years. Do you want the other statistics?

MILLY. Let's hear them.

DON. (*Picking up his pencil*.) Was it beer and sausages every Saturday night?

MILLY. Without fail.

DON. How many sausages?

MILLY. Two fat frankfritters each.

DON. One thousand and forty sausages. Beer?

MILLY. Also two bottles each.

DON. Say they hold a pint—exactly one hundred and thirty gallons of beer.

MILLY. Come again?

DON. One thousand and forty sausages and one hundred and thirty gallons of beer, to the nearest belch.

MILLY. Both of us, or just my share?

DON. Just your share.

MILLY. (*Emphatically, after a moment's reflection.*) It is *not* a lot. Not for ten years Don. It only sounds a lot. There were three thousand six hundred and fifty-two days remember!

DON. I can give it to you in hours.

MILLY. Yes! Let's hear that one.

DON. (*A pause while he works it out.* SHORTY *returns to the room.*) Eighty-seven thousand six hundred odd.

MILLY. *What!*

DON. Eighty seven thousand . . .

MILLY. Stop! I don't want to hear. (*Trembling with emotion.*) Jesus Christ, I wish I'd known that when he went out.

DON. For the sake of accuracy we'd better subtract sleeping time. The human being sleeps an average . . .

MILLY. What do you mean subtract? He got that as well. All right! So I've said it. He got the lot. Body and Soul. And me? A pile of sausages and a barrel of beer! You call that a bargain? (*Her mounting anger starts her pacing. She is still wearing the boxing gloves and will keep them on until, as indicated, after the bout with* SHORTY.) I must have been off my mind! There he stood ten years ago, on my threshold, with his suitcase of artificial roses—and I could have slammed the door in his face! I only bought a bunch out of pity. He gave me the old song and dance. Down and out, no friends, where's the next meal and all of this on the verge of tears. So open went the big heart and out came the helping hand. I'm telling you it was pity. That's the only reason why I went out with him to begin with. He looked lonely and as it so happened it was the end of his first week under my roof. "Dress up," he said. "Ve mus haf a celebrashin." And then they appeared! Those leather shorts with the bells and braces! Oh, my God! I nearly died of embarrassment. It was his legs! "You can't", I said. "I'm wearing white. They'll stare." "But ve ver dem in da mountince." That was him. Da mountince!

SHORTY. Switzerland.

MILLY. He's a German.

SHORTY. No Milly . . .

MILLY. I'm telling you he's a German. Look what they did to the Jews.

SHORTY. Mr. Ahlers says . . .

MILLY. Mister? He's just plain Ahlers in this house and what he says doesn't count because he's a liar, so shut up. Mister! (*Outraged.*) Listen, he was a hobo, an immigrant. He had nothing. If it wasn't for me he still wouldn't have a penny to scratch his backside with. I put the firm of Ahlers Artificial Flowers on its two flat feet that only had one pair of socks when they walked into my life. I typed the letters to the undertakers, and I'll give him notice.

DON. Tonight? When he comes home?

MILLY. Tonight.

DON. Want to bet?

SHORTY. What you betting?

DON. Beer and sausages at the Phoenix. (SHORTY *thinks this is very funny.*)

MILLY. When you're finished laughing, nitwit, I'd just like to remind you too what I said about somebody being the landlord around here and getting slowly sick to death. Think about it.

DON. (*To* SHORTY.) She's threatening us.

MILLY. I assure you it wouldn't break my heart.

SHORTY. What?

MILLY. To kick you out! A change in the faces around here would be as good as a holiday. . . . Quite frankly, I'd rather do away with myself than carry on like this.

DON. (*Picking up his pencil.*) How?

MILLY. Quick, because this is not worth it anymore. How many times have I laughed today? Not once. Not even a chuckle. And all the two of you can do is sit there and watch. Look at you now! For God's Sake Do Something!

SHORTY. (*Moving across to* MILLY *where he adopts*

a boxer's stance.) Put them up. I'll teach you to box.
(MILLY *stares at him silently for a few seconds then
lets loose a vicious swipe at his head. He dodges it
easily.*) That's it! Come on. (*He is now feinting and
weaving.* MILLY *tries a second swipe with the full in-
tention of hitting him.*) No Good!

MILLY. I'm warning you.

SHORTY. Okay.

MILLY. I'll knock you out!

SHORTY. Try. Come on. Try! (MILLY *goes after*
SHORTY, *swinging wildly.* SHORTY *puts up a great show.
Soon* MILLY *is enjoying herself immensely.*)

MILLY. I'll get you. Take that! And that! And that!
Wait! Stand still, you little bugger . . . ([*Etc.*]
Eventually SHORTY *deliberately lets* MILLY *connect.
He goes down.*) You're down! I told you! (*Laughing
freely she turns to* DON. *The look on his face stops
her laughter abruptly. She turns sharply on* SHORTY
who is still lying on the floor.) You trying to make
me happy?

SHORTY. You was laughing.

MILLY. It was a trick. (*Tearing off the gloves.*) Take
them.

SHORTY. Once more.

MILLY. Go to hell.

SHORTY. You did forget your troubles, Mill.

MILLY. Well, I don't want to forget. Not that way!
It was ten years. You think it's quits because you
make me laugh for ten seconds. Ten years! That's
what criminals get.

DON. Not again, Milly! . . .

MILLY. Yes, again! And again and again. And you're
going to listen. You're also on the face of this bloody
earth. I'll make you listen. I'll make you say it's all
wrong and he's bad and it isn't fair, because that's
what it is. Go on. Look! You. That. (*Indicating*
SHORTY.) This. (*Indicating the room.*) And me here
in the middle of the mess while he's out there spending

the profits I helped him earn on some cheap Jo'burg bitch.

DON. That's right.

MILLY. (*Outraged*.) Right?

DON. He's having a good time and you're forgotten. I told you that five minutes ago.

MILLY. So?

DON. So full stop. Finished. The end of a sad story.

MILLY. You mean he's going to get away with it?

DON. Why not? He hasn't broken the law. You're not married. He pays his rent. In the eyes of the law he's an innocent law-abiding citizen having what you call a good time.

MILLY. And in mine he's a low-down, rotten, stinking bastard, who has done something dirty and must be punished. And if nobody else is going to do it, I will. Tonight I will take my revenge.

DON. You tried once before and it didn't work.

MILLY. This time it will. We'll join forces. (*To* SHORTY.) Think!

SHORTY. What?

MILLY. Our plan for revenge.

SHORTY. I don't . . .

MILLY. Don't you want Sissy to be sorry she left you in the lurch?

SHORTY. Yes—

MILLY. And to promise she won't go out with other men?

SHORTY. Yes.

MILLY. Then shut up, and think.

SHORTY. Listen chaps. I think I'll go to bed.

MILLY. Stay where you are! You're in this too. Let's work it out. At this moment . . . come on, help me!

DON. You're forgotten.

MILLY. Right.

DON. They're laughing.

MILLY. Right.

DON. They're having a wonderful time and you're . . .

MILLY. All right! We've got the picture. Let's move on. They're going to come home. Expecting to find us at their mercy.

DON. Most likely.

MILLY. Waiting patiently.

DON. Willingly.

MILLY. Ready to crawl.

DON. Content with the crumbs.

MILLY. And that is when we strike. Because instead . . .

DON. Aha!

MILLY. And much to their surprise . . .

DON. It's coming!

MILLY. Much to their surprise, I repeat . . .

DON. Wait for it!

MILLY. I've got it! *They're* forgotten because *we* are having a good time. How's that? They walk in to find that we've forgotten all about them because we are laughing and singing and having a good time.

SHORTY. (*With pleasure.*) Hey!

MILLY. (*Warming to her idea.*) Because guess what's going full swing when they walk in through that front door? A party!

SHORTY. That don't sound so bad Milly.

MILLY. What do you say, Don?

DON. You've forgotten one thing. The party. Where does that come from?

MILLY. Us?

DON. You mean you, him, and me . . .

MILLY. . . . are going to have a party! Let me give you the picture this time. Half a bottle of Muscadel at the bottom of my wardrobe gets the ball rolling. We buy a cake, hang up some decorations. I've got all that stuff left over from Christmas. Let's be carefree man! Laughing and singing until the cows come home. And them upstairs having to endure it all the time.

Let's drive them mad. What do you say chaps?

SHORTY. That don't sound so bad at all Mill. I'm game.

DON. (*With signs of nervous wariness.*) You can't produce a party just like that, at this hour of the night, and out of thin air.

MILLY. I said we are going to have a party!

DON. To spite them?

MILLY. Yes.

DON. Well, it won't work. Nobody has a party to spite somebody else. Take my advice and drop the idea.

MILLY. *No.*

DON. For God's sake, Milly. Can't you see it? The three of us trying to be happy? We haven't got a reason. Try something else.

MILLY. You want a reason?

DON. Yes. Give me one good reason why the three of us . . .

MILLY. It's my birthday. (*Pause.*)

DON. I don't believe it.

MILLY. That amounts to calling me a liar.

DON. Let's just say you've made a mistake.

MILLY. And if I prove it? (*Pause.*) If I prove it the party's on. Right?

DON. I'm not saying anything.

MILLY. Well I'm saying it's my birthday and that I'm going to prove it . . .

DON. I'll buy you a present on Monday.

MILLY. We are going to celebrate my birthday with a party.

DON. Suppose it doesn't work? Suppose we don't have a good time?

MILLY. Leave that side of it to me.

DON. I've tried before.

MILLY. What's the matter with you, for God's sake? We're not going to try to do a miracle. A party! What are you scared of?

DON. I'm not scared of anything.

MILLY. You're trying to get out of it.

DON. Yes!

MILLY. Well you can't.

DON. There's no law which says I have to, you know. Well, is there? Let's just say I'm not in a party mood tonight. And anyway I'm no good at laughing or singing . . . you won't miss me. (*Pause. Growing embarrassment.*) Tell you what, I'll watch.

SHORTY. Hell, Don!

DON. Look, why am I so important? You two go ahead and . . .

MILLY. So this is the thanks I get.

SHORTY. There's nothing wrong with a party, Don.

MILLY. After all the friendship and encourgement I've given you.

SHORTY. Come on man! Say yes. For her sake.

DON. All right!

SHORTY. Yes?

DON. Yes. But I want it noted that I warned you. (*He sits.*)

MILLY. It's on. Anybody who backs out now is a deserter. And at the front line you get shot for that. (*To* SHORTY.) Get my bag. It's on my bed. (*Exit* SHORTY.) She who laughs last, laughs longest, and tonight I'll also make it loudest. I'll have him down here, on his knees, begging for mercy before the cock crows thrice. That's my vow. So help me God. (SHORTY *returns with the bag.* MILLY *takes out her purse.*) Take that . . . (*In a sudden fit of extravagance.*) . . . take the lot. Get us a cake. The best. Something mouthwatering. Cooldrinks, peanuts and raisins . . .

SHORTY. Potato crisps?

MILLY. The lot. It's got to look good. Well? What are you waiting for? Action stations.

(SHORTY *and* MILLY *moves to the door, leaving* DON *at the table.*)

CURTAIN

ACT TWO

The room is "decorated," the table has a cloth, plates, glasses, etc. In the center of the table is a candle stuck into a bottle. Curtain goes up to the sound of Milly *and* Don *arguing Offstage.* Don *is the first to appear.*

Don. No.

Milly. (*Close on his heels, carrying a long evening gown on a hanger.*) But it's an occasion.

Don. I prefer the one you're wearing.

Milly. Are you trying to be funny?

Don. Then let's just say the colour doesn't suit you.

Milly. Apricot.

Don. It's not in the spectrum.

Milly. Look at the sequins.

Don. Save up and buy a new one.

Milly. What do you mean? I've only worn this twice.

Don. So now it's out of fashion.

Milly. Since when?

Don. Donkey's years.

Milly. Listen to him!

Don. If you want my opinion . . .

Milly. I don't.

Don. . . . and you did ask for it, that garment is old-fashioned.

Milly. And I'm telling you it is not!

Don. They stopped wearing those before the war.

Milly. When you weren't even born yet, hey? (*Derisive laughter.*)

Don. Exactly! My mother had one just like it.

Milly. (*Laying it on thick.*) When you weren't even born yet! Ha ha! So kindly . . .

48

DON. I warn you if you wear that somebody will laugh.

MILLY. (*Unable to keep up the act.*) So kindly shut up!

DON. I've said what I wanted to. (*His pipe.*)

MILLY. *Shut up!* (*Exit with dress; returns immediately.*) I hope you took the hint and are going to do something about your appearance. You look a disgrace. (*Exit.*)

DON. (*Shouting.*) If Shorty doesn't come back soon you had better forget about a birthday party and call it a midnight supper! (MILLY *appears quietly in the doorway.* DON *doesn't see her. He shouts again.*) I said if Shorty doesn't return . . .

MILLY. I heard you! (*Pause.*) We've still got half an hour. As long as we start before twelve it's valid. (*Pause.*) Worse comes to the worst we can start without him. So get ready.

DON. Just the two of us? Are you mad? (*Pause.* MILLY *stands quite still. So does* DON.)

MILLY. If he gets back too late I'll kill him. This is a hell of an end of my year. I won't scream, but I think I'm loosing my hold. (*Front door opens.* SHORTY *rushes breathless into the room.*)

SHORTY. I've got everything Mill. Hey, this looks good!

MILLY. You know how close you've brought us to disaster?

SHORTY. Disaster?

MILLY. Stop wasting time and give me the grub. Hurry up. It's touch and go now. (SHORTY *puts on the lights,* MILLY *blows out the candle and then sorts out the parcels* SHORTY *has brought back. Out of one she takes a bunch of beetroot leaves.*) What's this? (SHORTY *laughs.*) I'm asking you what is this?

SHORTY. Beetroot leaves, for the silkies. That's why I took a little bit long Mill. I went to that shop . . .

MILLY. Right! We'll settle that with this. (*She slaps*

SHORTY's *face and then throws the leaves out of the window.*)

SHORTY. Why did you do that?

MILLY. Never you mind why. It helped. (*Turning back to the parcels.*) Where's the cake? (SHORTY *hands her a parcel which she opens.*) And this? (*She holds up a slab-cake.*)

SHORTY. Cake.

MILLY. But it's slab-cake (SORTY *examines his purchase.*) I didn't ask for slab-cake, idiot.

SHORTY. He said it's fruitcake.

MILLY. I wanted a round cake.

SHORTY. You didn't say nothing to me about a round cake, Milly. Did she, Don?

MILLY. Who the hell ever heard of a birthday party with slab-cake. What can I do with this? A few crumby slices. It's supposed to be wedges with icing. (*Throwing the cake onto the table.*) No! That does it. (*Walks away and lights a cigarette.*)

DON. So what is happening?

SHORTY. Slap me again. Hard as you like.

DON. Are you calling it off?

MILLY. (*Turning back to the table.*) Now listen! Both of you! Just once more, you understand. So help me God, either of you just once more and you'll regret the day you were born. (*To* SHORTY.) Get a plate. Come on, move! (*Indicating the half bottle of muscadel.*) There's only one tot each so don't make pigs of yourselves. Sip it.

DON. I want it noted that I am going into this under protest.

MILLY. And without any improvement in your appearance! (*To* SHORTY.) Put off the light. (*He does so after she has lit the candle.*) Ready? (*Each of them is standing behind a chair.*) All together! (*They sit.*) No, wait! Stand.

DON. Make up your mind. (*They stand.* MILLY *exits hurriedly and returns with a few paper hats.*)

MILLY. Last Christmas, but he'll never remember. Take one.

DON. Is this compulsory?

MILLY. Yes.

SHORTY. (*Singing.*) For she's a jolly good fellow, for she's a jolly good fellow, for she's a jolly good fellow, and so say all of us.

MILLY. All right. Sit. Together. (*They sit.*)

SHORTY. To Milly, and may she live happily ever after. (*Glasses are touched, they drink. Pause.*)

MILLY. And now?

DON. You're supposed to make a speech.

MILLY. No.

SHORTY. You must make a speech on your birthday, Milly.

MILLY. A few words then, but no speech. (*She stands.*) Well . . . (*Pause.*) No. (*She sits.*)

SHORTY. Come on, Mill.

DON. Reply to the toast.

MILLY. All right. I'm prepared to do that. I'll reply to the toast. (*Stands again.*) God, I feel a fool! (*Pulling herself together.*) Anyway, I'm happy—no, let's not exaggerate—I'm pleased to be here with you. Or rather, to have you here with me. It's my house, remember. It's also my birthday. I'm not an old woman by any manner of means. But I've seen a lot of life. Just don't get any ideas, because there's plenty left. The spirit is willing even though the flesh be weak. I'm not talking about Sin. I mean life, and it's taken its toll. Somebody once said you start to die the moment you are born. The fact remains however that the best years are the middle years, somebody else said. I side with him. Because the spirit *is* willing even . . . though . . . back to the beginning! But of a knot. Anyway, I hope you know that I know what I mean. Which is, there are plenty of kicks left in the old girl! So what else? No one could call me mean. Share and share alike has always been my motto. I've never begrudged you second helpings or clean sheets. I've tried to make this a home for you boys. Furthermore, Shorty, I don't hate you. But you do get on my nerves sometimes, quite honestly. Try and behave yourself more. I'm not strict, but I hate fools. Really I do. As for you, Don, for God's sake, man, buck up your ideas a little. Do something. Get a girl or see a skin specialist but do something. I also hate layabouts. That seems to cover everything. No! one more thing. Let's try and be more cheerful in future. What do you say? Postboxes and pimples aren't the end of the world, chaps. So let's brighten up with a few more smiles. Let's make that the resolution. (MILLY *sits. Applause from* SHORTY *and* DON.)

SHORTY. Very good, Mill! Very good!

MILLY. Thank you.

SHORTY. Hip hip hooray! (*Still clapping.*) Blow, man! Blow! Its your birthday.

(*Carried away by the flush of success* MILLY *leans forward and blows out the candle, plunging them in darkness. Silence.*)

MILLY. That wasn't very clever of you, was it? (*Pause.*) So find the matches! (*Fumbling in the dark. A bottle is knocked over, something falls to the floor.*) Watch out, you clumsy ape!

SHORTY. I got them. (*Match flares, the candle is lit.* MILLY *examines the table.*)

MILLY. Just look at this mess! No. We'll start again.

DON. Another speech?

MILLY. From scratch.

DON. But the booze is finished. We can't toast you with cooldrink. For better or worse, we've reached the cutting of the cake.

MILLY. Let's at least tidy up. (*The table is tidied.*)

DON. Cut the cake. I'm hungry.

SHORTY. Same here. (MILLY *cuts the slab of fruit-*

*cake, putting a slice on each plate. They begin to eat
and drink. Apart from an occasional grunt of satisfaction, not a word is spoken.* MILLY *eats slowly, with
affectation.* DON *and* SHORTY *pile in. They quickly
finish their first slice.* MILLY *cuts again. The cooldrinks
are opened, the potato crisps disappear, then the peanuts. Not a word is spoken.* DON *and* SHORTY *hold out
their plates for more cake.*)

MILLY. Not so fast!

DON. I'm peckish.

MILLY. You're wolfing. (*She cuts two more slices.*
DON *and* SHORTY *continue eating.* MILLY *now begins
to realize something is going wrong. She eats slower
and slower, eventually stopping altogether to watch
the other two with growing frustration and disgust.
When just about everything has been eaten,* DON
pushes back his chair and belches.)

DON. An old Arab custom which means Thank you.

SHORTY. Hear, hear.

MILLY. You mean!

DON. The party. Wasn't as bad as I expected quite
frankly.

MILLY. It's finished? It's over.

DON. Isn't it?

MILLY. No it's not. We haven't even started.

DON. What's left? We've eaten the cake . . .

SHORTY. There's still some cheese-tips here.

MILLY. The fun for God's sake!

DON. Fun?

MILLY. Don't pretend you know nothing about it.
(*Pause. She looks at them.*) The sound of merry
laughter.

DON. In here? Us?

MILLY. That was the agreement.

DON. I thought it was too good to be true.

SHORTY. I think we had some fun Milly.

MILLY. Merry laughter!

SHORTY. I laughed. Ask Don.

MILLY. You smirked once with shame because I caught you with your gob stuffed full of food.

DON. (*Wearily*.) So there hasn't been any fun. So what!

MILLY. Well there's going to be. That's what. I'm throwing this party because I want to laugh. Understand? He's going to hear me laughing when he comes back. So this party is not yet over. Nobody goes to bed until I've laughed! (*She lights a cigarette and smokes*.)

SHORTY. I've got a joke.

DON. No. Don't let's start that.

MILLY. Tell it.

DON. This is courting disaster Milly. Believe me. Jokes . . .

MILLY. Tell it!

SHORTY. It's rude.

MILLY. We're not babies.

SHORTY. What's the difference between an ostrich egg and an ordinary egg?

MILLY. That's not a joke.

SHORTY. George called it a joke.

MILLY. It's a riddle you idiot. A riddle doesn't make you laugh.

DON. What's the answer?

SHORTY. An arse-stretch.

MILLY. Apologize! Apologize for that immediately!

SHORTY. Sorry.

DON. Satisfied?

MILLY. Will you stop trying to make me satisfied with nothing.

DON. I think we had a fair run for our money.

MILLY. We've had one dirty riddle, and the spectacle of you gutsing yourself on *my* money.

DON. If I pay you back my share will you call it quits?

MILLY. You'll pay me back your share by making me laugh.

Don. Milly, please! I'm being serious.

Milly. That makes two of us.

Don. I know, and that's why I'm nervous. It won't work. Take my advice and call it a day. Nothing's happened yet . . .

Milly. Exactly!

Don. (*Trying to ignore her.*) . . . we're intact, in shape. We can still retire with grace. But beyond this lies the point of no return.

Milly. Good! I've always hated going back.

Don. For the last time I'm warning you—this is getting dangerous.

Milly. Coward!

Don. All right.

Milly. Yellow belly!

Don. (*Standing.*) If that's the way you feel about it, I'll leave the two of you . . .

Milly. Just you try! (Don *stops.*) Just you try!

Shorty. (*Trying to pour oil on troubled waters.*) Please chaps.

Milly. (*To* Don.) So sit down and shut up, because here we go. (*With growing aggression.*) To start off with, there'll be a sing-song.

Don. I flatly refuse.

Shorty. Don, please, man!

Milly. We'll start the ball rolling with a sing-song. (*Stubs out her cigarette and lights another. She is now grimly determined.*) What songs do you know, Shorty?

Shorty. "Pack up your troubles in your old kit-bag and Smile, Smile, Smile."

Milly. One, two, three! (*Singing.*) "Pack up your troubles in your old kit-bag and smile boys, that's the stuff . . . (Shorty *joins in.*)
What's the use of wor-ree-ying,
It only gets you down,
Soooo—pack up your troubles in your old kit-bag and Smile, Smile, Smile."

SHORTY. We did sing that in the lorry going to Military Camp Mill!

MILLY. Next one, "Roll out the barrel." Sing! (SHORTY *and* MILLY *sing.*)

"Roll out the barrel
We'll have a barrel of fun
Roll out the barrel
Ta ta, te ta ta, tum tum . . ." I forget the words.

SHORTY. Same here.

MILLY.   "Jerusalem!"   (*Singing.*)   "Ja-roo-sa-lem . . ."

SHORTY. I don't know that one Mill!

MILLY. What about "When Irish eyes are Smiling?"

SHORTY. I'll try. Come on, Don! (SHORTY *and* MILLY *sing.*) "Sure the world seems bright and gay . . . for when Irish eyes are smiling . . ."

(DON, *who has sat tensed through the foregoing, making no attempt to help the other two, now jumps to his feet.* MILLY, *blinded by determination, does not see the impending catastrophe. There is from this point on, a growing momentum to the final chaos, with everybody cutting into or talking over someone else's words.*)

DON. This is a fiasco!

MILLY. Almost chaps. Almost!

DON. Officially . . .

MILLY. We're nearly there!

SHORTY. Mario Lanza!

DON. Officially this is now a fiasco . . .

MILLY. Once more and we'll make it!

DON. I can't stand it any longer.

MILLY. Then sit down and sing!

DON. There are fates worse than death.

MILLY. (*Closing her eyes.*) "Smiling Through!"

SHORTY. But you isn't even trying, Don.

DON. Because I don't want to.

SHORTY. No, Don. You must sing.

DON. Are you deaf? I Don't Want To . . . !

SHORTY. Shame on you, Don! It's her birthday.

MILLY. (*Her eyes still closed.*) I said "Smiling Through." On your marks, get set, GO. (*Singing.*) "There's a little grey road winding over the hill, to a little white house by the sea . . ." ([*Etc.*] DON *and* SHORTY *continue their argument over this.*)

DON. Well, she can have it. Just leave me . . .

SHORTY. No, Don.

DON. . . . leave me out of it.

SHORTY. No, Don, that's not fair.

DON. I don't care if it's not!

SHORTY. I say you must sing, because . . .

DON. And I'm saying . . . (DON *and* SHORTY *erupt simultaneously into protestations and accusations.* MILLY *is still singing her song, in her loudest voice, with her eyes tightly closed. Bedlam. At the height of the racket she picks up a spoon and starts banging on the table.*)

MILLY. Order! Order! (*The argument continues;* MILLY *hammers away.*) Order, I say!

DON. I warned you this was going to happen. I refuse to take the blame for this fiasco.

SHORTY. Well, it wasn't me, because I was singing.

MILLY. You're out of order. Both of you come to order at once! (*Silence.*) We won't get anywhere by shouting. (*She is speaking with a supreme effort at control and deliberation.*) I know it's serious, but we must keep calm if we hope to get to the bottom of . . . this . . . In fact I think we're already there. Speaking from experience, I'd say this was rock bottom. I've never known it harder. Keep cool. I'm coming to the point. Hidden in all this confusion is a Crime—a serious criminal offence. I demand Justice! (*Pause.*) I can't show you blood or bruises. The victim isn't even dead. But that won't stop me now from looking at you, and you, and pronouncing you two bastards, Guilty!

DON. (*Held by the accusation.*) And you?

MILLY. Your victim.

SHORTY. What we done this time, Milly?

MILLY. Tonight.

DON. And you're accusing *us?*

MILLY. Yes.

DON. *We're* to blame?

MILLY. I want to say it again . . .

DON. No.

MILLY. Guilty!

DON. No! I tried to stop you. I warned you—every inch of the way. But you wouldn't listen. *You* wanted a party.

MILLY. Yes. A bit of mirth. Sing out the old and laugh in the new. A few chuckles. Is that making impossible demands? This was my birthday.

SHORTY. But what was wrong with it?

MILLY. What do you call this? Slabcake and pimples, cigarette butts and silkworms, and nothing to do?

SHORTY. It wasn't so bad, Mill.

MILLY. Is this all you want?

SHORTY. I'm happy.

MILLY. You're not.

SHORTY. But I am.

MILLY. Well you've got no right to be. And if you're too stupid to see why, I'll tell you. And to start off with let me tell you to your face that I don't like you. As true as God is my witness, looking at you now I can say I don't like the sight of you. You nauseate me. He teases you. He's teasing you all the time, and I'm disgusted.

SHORTY. I don't mind a few jokes.

MILLY. There's only one. You. You're the joke. Sissy was right. You're ugly and a joke and I'm filled with shame to find you doing all this to mankind under my roof. Do you understand now. Must I say it again? We find you revolting. Ask him. (*She smokes violently.*)

SHORTY. (*To* DON.) She's joking.

MILLY. (*To* DON.) Tell him. (*Pause.*) Coward! Funk!

DON. What do you hope to gain from all this?

MILLY. The truth. I want you down here—rock bottom where you belong. Are you scared?

DON. No.

MILLY. Well, he's waiting to hear it.

DON. I study you, Shorty.

MILLY. He thinks you're a curiosity.

DON. It's in the interest of Science.

MILLY. Get to the point.

DON. You see, you're what they mean by simpleminded.

MILLY. He once called you a perfect specimen of a retarded poor white.

DON. Overseas you'd be a labourer—digging up the streets in London.

MILLY. No you don't! You said he'd be emptying the dirtbins in Birmingham.

DON. Here we have Natives to do the dirty work. You're saved by your white skin. Because examine the facts. You can just about read and write. You can't carry out the simple duties of a postman. I don't think you could do anything complicated. You blunder on from day to day with a weak defence—yet you survive. You even have a wife.

MILLY. Aha!

DON. I'm amazed at your survival. According to Darwin you should be dead. That's all.

MILLY. No it's not. You've left out the best bit of the lot. Sissy. Tell him what we whisper.

DON. I don't think she's properly your wife.

MILLY. Don't be clever. He's a simple-minded poor-white, remember.

DON. I don't think you know how.

MILLY. (*To* SHORTY.) Do you understand? He doesn't think you know how to do it. I think you do, but that Sissy doesn't want it from you, because we *both* think that Billy knows how. (*They watch* SHORTY *intently.*)

SHORTY. I'll hit you, Don!

MILLY. Bravo!

SHORTY. 'S true's there's a God, I'll hit you.

MILLY. And me? What will you do to me?

SHORTY. If you was a man I'd hit you too.

MILLY. And Billy?

SHORTY. I'll bugger up the lot of you.

MILLY. Now we're getting somewhere. The rock-bottom boxing match! Get out your gloves and hit! But first! . . . let's tell him if he wants to see a real psychological curiosity to have a good look in the mirror next time he squeezes his pimples. That's why no decent, clean-living girl will ever stomach the sight of you. Furthermore, you also blow your nose on the sheets, I've seen you use the washbasin in the bathroom as a W.C., and I've a strong suspicion that, as regards positively filthy habits, that is still not the worst. Sometimes when I think of your hands I want to vomit. And he's looking for himself! Take my advice— Don't! You'll be disgusted when you find it. Who do you think you're fooling? Calling him a freak! You're a washout.

DON. You finished?

MILLY. If you've hit the bottom with a bump— Yes.

DON. Because there's a few things that could be said about you.

MILLY. Go ahead. It's a free-for-all.

DON. (*To* SHORTY.) Come on. Let's tell her.

MILLY. Christ, you're yellow.

DON. You've started to get old woman odours. You should use scent. It's unpleasant being near you at times. That's why I've got no appetite left. And maybe that's why Ahlers doesn't want to marry you. Yes! You're also not fooling anybody. I guessed it long ago. And quite frankly I don't blame him. Because the thought of living intimately with you for the rest of my life, in the same room . . . !

MILLY. So I'm also ugly. What does that prove?

DON. As much as you've proved against us. Nothing.

MILLY. But I'm accusing you of desertion. That's my charge. That in the hour of need, in the thick of the fight, you deserted a fellow human being who had her back to the wall in a tight corner. Because I'll say it again . . . I tried!

DON. You won't get a medal for that. I also got out of bed. I also breathed, and walked and scratched myself . . . and all the other heroisms. Shorty, too. We suffered the same fate. We're also victims.

MILLY. Then prove it.

DON. How?

MILLY. By crying. Come on. Shed one tear and I'll believe you.

DON. Have you?

MILLY. Yes! Twice today I went to the W. C., pulled the chain so nobody would hear, and wept! But you two? (*Mimicking them.*) "It's not so bad, Mill." "Let's call it a day." Is this all we get?

DON. (*With sudden vehemence.*) Yes! It's all you get. And what's more you've had it. It's nearly twelve o'clock and then you're a year older. And there's not many more left where that one came from. You're in the home stretch, Milly!

MILLY. (*Summoning up all her control to ask the question for the last time.*) You are telling me this is all I get?

DON. Yes!

MILLY. (*Almost a cry.*) Then somebody's a bloody liar. Because there were promises. The agreement was that it would be worth it. Well, it isn't. I've been cheated. The whole thing was just a trick to get me to go on. Otherwise who would? Who wants to get up tomorrow if this is it? If this is all? Fifty years! That's a lot of patience. Nobody's so well off that fifty years doesn't leave him hard-up for what's left. I am. I'm broke. So I want what I'm owed. Pay up or be damned. (*Pause.* SHORTY *and* DON *stare at* MILLY. *Her resolution has reached its climax and now begins to ebb.*) Why? That's it! That's all. I just want to know why. It's not a silly question. When you lie in the dark and ask, and listen, it sounds like sense, like there should be an answer. Why? Why me? Why this? (DON *and* SHORTY *are still staring at her.*) Go on they said. It's good for you. Go on. Grow up! They all seemed happy with it back in old Pringle Street. So I believed them. I was young. And . . . (*Pause, after which she continues softly, her voice charged with amazement.*) I was young! Yes. Come to think of it. Me. Once . . . Pringle Street. Number nineteen, near the top. And a time, so young! a day, one special day that was eleven years old in one-way Pringle Street. It was dark. It was Sunday night and getting dark and Basil my best friend was stamping cockroaches under the lamp-post. So I said "Shame on you Basil!" But he said they didn't feel because there wasn't any blood. I was sitting on our wall singing "When you Wish upon a star, makes no matter what you are." Usually there was something sad about Sundays because of Monday and School. But this time it was holidays and altogether different. I was thinking about this and then slowly I began to grow happy. The darker it got the happier I grew. So I sang my song again and wanted to cry it was so big. And that night for the first time I beat Basil to the lamp-post when the light went on. He was so busy stamping cockroaches he didn't see. So I ran and touched it first and shouted "My Wish! My Wish!" Basil got jealous and said wishes didn't come true. But I just laughed at him. Because you know what I wished? Happiness! All those holidays it kept coming. You were right about the dress, Don —white. But you forgot the bell. There was a bell once. It was after Sunday School and I was running home singing "All things bright and beautiful . . ." and there was this bell. Oh, my God! This bell was ringing, chaps! And I was running in that sun shining

the way it should singing "All things bright and
beautiful, all creatures great and small!" How's that
for faith? With all the heart of eleven years old I
believed it, that it was mine, and forever. Because
I wished. Every time, every chance—falling stars,
black cats, white horses—every wish was Happiness!
. . . I had it. That night I mean . . . Happiness. It
felt like I was holding it so tight it was forever and
ever. But my hands! Mildred Constance Jenkins. Fifty
years old . . . I'm not a woman any more . . . he
says. I never thought of it like that, but he says I'm
not a woman any more. Last week it was, one night.
He was eating liver sausage in bed and I just told
him, you know, in case he started wondering. Then he
said, matter-of-fact I'll admit, not meaning to hurt,
that therefore strictly speaking I'm not a woman any
more. It sounded logical the way he put it. To do with
function. The function of a thing, and being a woman,
that meant babies. And you see, suddenly he sat up
and said he wanted a family! Because of the business
and Ahlers being a good name to keep alive through
the ages. We better stop now, he said. But we can
still be friends. So you see it's gone. Or just about. A
little left but mostly in the way of time. The rest just
Gone. Not broken, or stolen, or violated—which might
make it sound like there's been no crime, I know. But
I did have it and now it's gone and nobody ever gets
it back so don't tell me that doesn't make us victims.
Don't ask me how! Somehow! Victims of something.
Looks at us. All flesh and bone, with one face hanging
onto your neck until you're dead! (*Inside the house
the clock begins to chime. They listen in silence for a
few seconds, then . . .*) Ignore that! Where were we?
Today! What was I saying? Today . . . today . . .
Hold on! This one I won't let go! Today, today . . .
All right! You win, damn you. Yesterday! (*The clock
mechanism is again at fault. It chimes on and on and
on. Exit.* SHORTY *a blow Offstage stops the chiming.*

MILLY *softly*.) Mildred Jenkins you are still alive!

SHORTY. (*He returns*.) Sunday!

MILLY. So let's sort it out. To begin with don't take what I said too seriously. I got excited—flushed—if you really want to know. Hot and bothered. It's a symptom. We'll survive. Also, if anyone asks, meaning you know who, let's all say we had a good time in the form of a quiet gathering. (*Pause*.) That's all. (SHORTY *goes up to* MILLY.) Well?

SHORTY. You said you hate me.

MILLY. I exaggerated.

SHORTY. So you like me?

MILLY. No need to go to the other extreme. Let's just say you're also human and leave it at that. "Bury the hatchet on Sunday, dig it up on Monday."

SHORTY. So we're all friends again. Okay, Don?

DON. Okay, Shorty.

SHORTY. Shake. (*They shake*.) Milly, I got an idea.

MILLY. You keep trying I'll say that for you.

SHORTY. The zoo.

MILLY. It's cruel to keep living things behind bars.

SHORTY. What about us going tomorrow? It will be fun, man, George says there's a baboon with a blue bum who hates us.

MILLY. I think I remember him.

SHORTY. Everybody laughs, and then he gets cross.

MILLY. (*In indignation*.) Do you blame him? No, really! I think that's going too far.

SHORTY. What?

MILLY. For God's sake! Blue? How would you feel? Honestly, sometimes, some of the shapes . . . ! I wonder if creation knows what it's up to. I'll have a good look at that poor bastard tomorrow.

DON. (*Quoting the hymn*.)
"All creatures great and small
  The Lord God made them all."

MILLY. But Bright and Beautiful! That's how the hymn starts. Blue might be bright, but it's not beautiful *there*. Oh no.

SHORTY. We'll have a good look, Milly.

MILLY. God help you if you laugh.

SHORTY. I won't, I promise.

MILLY. Because it's not funny.

SHORTY. So can I get my leaves?

MILLY. It's pathetic.

SHORTY. Leaves, Milly!

MILLY. Leaves? What leaves? It's winter.

SHORTY. To feed my silkies. You threw them away.

MILLY. So I did. Feed them by all means. I hope they're crisp.

SHORTY. They're still on the pavement. I seen them (*Exit.*)

MILLY. (*To* DON.) He means well. The heart's good. It's the mentality that's weak.

DON. (*Standing.*) To bed, to sleep, perchance no dreams.

MILLY. Not yet. Coffee. Drown our sorrows in the dregs.

DON. (*Sitting.*) Here we go again.

MILLY. (*Laughing.*) Into the Valley of Death! Know that one?

DON. "The Lord is my shepherd. Yea though I walk."

MILLY. Never! The charge of the Light Brigade. "Into the Valley of Death rode the gallant four hundred."

DON. It's the same valley.

SHORTY. (*He returns and goes to a shelf at the back. Going to the table with his shoebox.*) Guess what, chaps? They're all in silk. I don't need the leaves now Milly. Look! One is still spinning.

MILLY. (*Looking at the shoebox.*) So that's how they do it! Congratulations, Shorty. Well done! What happens now?

SHORTY. Now?

MILLY. With them. (SHORTY *looks to* DON *for guidance.*) The next step.

SHORTY. I don't know. Nothing.

MILLY. But the moths. Moths are going to come out. Isn't that so, Don?

SHORTY. I don't want moths.

MILLY. Well that's just too bad, because you're going to get them.

SHORTY. Nobody keeps the moths.

MILLY. So tell me what happens to them!

SHORTY. I don't know.

DON. Don't start again.

MILLY. Don what happens to the moths?

DON. We've had enough questions for one night, Milly!

MILLY. Will somebody kindly tell me what happens to the moths?

DON. (*At breaking point.*) I don't know and I don't care and as far as I am concerned . . .

MILLY. (*With mounting indignation.*) Now just hang on! There's something wrong here. I smell that rat again. (*To* SHORTY.) Why have you been feeding them?

SHORTY. It was Jossie who . . .

MILLY. Why Have You Kept Them Alive?

SHORTY. To see them spin. To see the silk.

MILLY. And now that they've done it, they've had it. Is that it?

SHORTY. (*Desperate.*) I don't know all about this, Milly!

MILLY. You're going to chuck them away.

SHORTY. Okay. I'll keep them and watch the moths.

MILLY. To starve! To die!

DON. (*Unable to take any more.*) For Christ's sake what do you want?

MILLY. (*With equal violence.*) Some other way! Don't you? Must it always be the muckheap? Isn't there another solution?

DON. Then find it!

MILLY. I will.

SHORTY. Hang on, Don. Look, Milly . . . As God is

my witness I'll feed them. They'll get fat. (DON *gets up. Thinking he is making a move to his room,* MILLY *jumps in front of the backdoor and stands there spread-eagled, blocking his exit.*)

MILLY. Where do you think you're going?

DON. Come with. You can hold my hand. Come! (*Exit into the passage where the lavatory door slams.* MILLY *rushes to the doorway and shouts after him.*)

MILLY. You've got a dirty brain, Donovan Brad-shaw! (MILLY *turning back into the room she finds* SHORTY *staring at her.*) Feed them! (*She starts to clear the table. The front door opens. A disconsolate* SISSY *appears in the passage doorway.*)

SHORTY. Hello, Siss.

SISSY. (*Noticing the decorations.*) What's going on here?

SHORTY. We had a party.

SISSY. With dancing?

MILLY. (*Before* SHORTY *can reply.*) Singing, dancing, drinking. The lot.

SISSY. Is it finished?

MILLY. Yes! We had a good time and it's finished. So you missed it. (*Exit.*)

SISSY. You didn't say nothing to me about a party!

SHORTY. It was a surprise party. Even we didn't know. It was Milly's birthday. Say Happy Birthday when she comes back.

SISSY. No.

SHORTY. It's sad, Siss. She's unhappy.

SISSY. Well, so am I.

SHORTY. Wasn't it a good picture?

SISSY. Who all was at the party?

SHORTY. Just us. Me and Don and Milly.

SISSY. That doesn't sound so hot.

SHORTY. It was okay. But . . . (*Whispering.*) We didn't dance. (*Pause.*) We discussed. (*Pause.*) Sissy I don't want you to see Billy any more.

SISSY. Same here.

SHORTY. Why?

SISSY. You mean are all the same.

SHORTY. But I'm your husband.

SISSY. That's your lookout.

SHORTY. (*Pointing to the shoe box on the table.*)
They're all in silk now, Sissy.

SISSY. What do I care.

SHORTY. I'll wait for the moths.

SISSY. I don't want moths in the room. They'll eat
my clothes. I only got a few, for your information.

SHORTY. I'll keep them here in the kitchen. Milly
likes moths.

SISSSY. God help you if you bring them into the
room.

SHORTY. I won't, I promise.

SISSY. You always promise but nothing comes true.
We been married six months now and just look. You're
lucky I didn't know.

SHORTY. Don't say that, Siss.

SISSY. Well then, do something!

SHORTY. (*Really desperate.*) But what? What must
a guy do? I slog.

SISSY. Let's go away from here.

SHORTY. Aren't we happy here?

SISSY. I'm not. They don't like me. You don't protect
me you know. You let them scandal about me.

SHORTY. Where do you want to go?

SISSY. How must I know? (*Pause.*) Somewhere nice.

SHORTY. Shamley Boarding house?

SISSY. Back there! Are you mad? (*Pause.*) Cape
Town.

SHORTY. Cape Town? *Cape Town.*

SISSY. You asked me, so I'm telling you.

SHORTY. But what about my job?

SISSY. Ask them to transfer you.

SHORTY. (*With finality.*) I know nothing about
transfers Sissy.

SISSY. Well ask them. Ask George.

SHORTY. But I don't know the streets down there, Siss! I'll never get the letters right. Please, not Cape Town.

SISSY. So must it be Braamfontein all my life?

SHORTY. Sissy . . . (*Pause.*)

SISSY. Hurry up. I haven't got all night.

SHORTY. Don't be unhappy, because . . . something happens.

SISSY. What?

SHORTY. It's to do with getting old.

SISSY. So?

SHORTY. We get old.

SISSY. What you talking about?

SHORTY. I don't know. I'm all mixed up. But it was so clear.

SISSY. You're mad.

SHORTY. No, ask Milly. She told us. Promises don't come true . . .

SISSY. That's not news to me with you around.

SHORTY. . . . and we get old.

SISSY. You've already said that.

SHORTY. But we're young.

SISSY. So what?

SHORTY. You mustn't be frightened. S'true's God, I'm your husband.

SISSY. All right!

SHORTY. So let's go to bed.

SISSY. I'm tired.

SHORTY. Okay. Come.

SISSY. I'm very tired tonight.

SHORTY. But we got it, Sissy. Truly. By Special Licence. It's okay. They all say it's as good as in a Church.

SISSY. Have you been discussing my private life in public?

SHORTY. I just want you to be brave. Let's go.

SISSY. Just remember I'm tired. I want to go to sleep. Understand?

SHORTY. Come.

SISSY. Do you understand?

SHORTY. I'm also tired.

SISSY. Do You Understand? (*Pause.*)

SHORTY. (*Defeated.*) Yes.

SISSY. Because I'm warning you. If you do I'll call for help again. (*She moves to the door.* SHORTY *following. Before they reach it they are stopped by* MILLY's *voice, loud and urgent.*)

MILLY. (*Offstage, hammering on the lavatory door.*) Don! Hurry up! All hands on deck. You've got five seconds at the most! (*She now enters the room highly excited, and finds* SHORTY *and* SISSY *near the door.*) Get back! Sit down!

SHORTY. What's going on, Mill?

MILLY. Sit down, I say!

(*A few seconds of furious activity, during which she piles empty bottles and plates on the table, rushes out for something and then grabs a glass and fills it up with cooldrink. In between all this she forces* SISSY *and* SHORTY *into chairs, urging them to "Smile"—"Grab a glass"—" Look Happy," etc.* DON *appears in the doorway.*)

DON. What's happened?

MILLY. Ahlers! He's coming up the road. Sit down. Now, all together . . .

DON. No.

MILLY. . . . laugh!

DON. For heaven's sake, Milly!

MILLY. My sake, damn you! Sit down. Laugh you bas . . . (*The front doors opens.*) Ha ha ha ha ha! (*Hissing.*) Come on! (SHORTY *tries to help.*) Ha ha ha ha ha! Very good! Drink up, chaps! Empty the bottles. Polish off those savouries. Ha ha ha! My God, that's a killer! Ostrich Eggs! One of the best jokes I've heard in years! (*Drifting towards ther door. Then*

*when she gets there she holds up her hand for silence
as if the party was an uproar of merriment and noise.)*
Hang on chaps! Hang on! Come and see what the cat's
dragged in. If you asked me, I'd say that a certain old
friend from the Fatherland turned out to be a bit of
a flop. *(Now speaking directly to Ahlers in the passage.)* What happened? She say you were too old
for her? You are, you know. Just don't think that
means you can come crawling back to me. Because I
had a damn good time without you. Didn't we boys?
(Ahlers is now moving up the stairs. MILLY *shifts her
position.)* So don't start banging on the floor at four
o'clock if we're still going strong. This happens to be
my house! Let's get that straight. And don't bother to
ask if you can join in, because you can't. (MILLY
moves out of sight into the passage.) And finally, let
me tell you nothing is finished. I've proved it. You
never had anything to do with it anyway. You're not
God. You're a parasite. A bloodsucking Hitler! *(A
door slams.)* That's right, shut your door. But you'll
still hear me! *(She is back in the kitchen now and
shouting up at the ceiling.)* If it's the last thing I do,
I'll make you hear me! *(To the others.)* Sing! Come
on! *(Singing.)* "Why was she born so . . ." *Come on!*
(SHORTY *is again the only one who tries to help.)*
"Why was she born so beautiful, Why was she born at
all!" *(Silence.* MILLY *lights a cigarette and takes a
few draws. To* SHORTY *and* SISSY.) Party's over. Bugger off. *(To* DON.) Not you. *(Exit* SHORTY *and* SISSY.)
You think he believed it?

DON. Do you want my honest opinion?

MILLY. No! But I bet you anything you like there's
doubt. That's even worse. I just hope it gnaws.

DON. You didn't give him notice.

MILLY. I will.

DON. You said tonight. We took a bet.

MILLY. Play my trump card just like that! Don't
be a fool!

DON. Milly . . .

MILLY. If you were up in the trenches would you blast off all your ammo at one go?

DON. Milly! Milly! There aren't any trenches. This is Hospital Hill, Braamfontein.

MILLY. Well if these aren't hostilities, I'd like to know what are.

DON. It can't last forever, Milly.

MILLY. What?

DON. You and him.

MILLY. Forever! Who said anything about that. I'm halfway there anyway.

DON. So what do you hope to win?

MILLY. Tomorrow. (*Pause.*)

DON. (*Helplessly.*) I don't know.

MILLY. That's right.

DON. I'm tired. Declare an armistice.

MILLY. What for?

DON. Then we can sleep in peace tonight.

MILLY. Peace! You can talk about peace in times like these? Are you mad? Some nights when I lie in bed and those ambulances go screaming past and I think: More Casualties! . . . I can just about smell the cannon smoke. Anyway, I couldn't sleep with him still stomping around. Last eye open in an old house . . . that's me!

DON. Suppose his doubt gnaws away all night?

MILLY. If that happens, I'm a happy woman.

DON. But if he doesn't go to bed?

MILLY. We hang on. Keep the fort. It's worth waiting for.

DON. We?

MILLY. You're in this up to your neck.

DON. I know. I drowning.

MILLY. Then call for help. That'll keep you awake if the coffee doesn't work. No point in going under half asleep.

DON. I can't, Milly.

MILLY. What?

DON. Call for help.

MILLY. (*Briskly.*) Go on! (*She moves, but stops after a few steps to stare at* DON.) What's this now?

DON. I'm dumb. When things happen, I watch. Even when it's to myself . . . all I do is watch. I used to think the right word for me was Numb . . . that there wasn't even Feeling. But I think that's wrong. I'm sure if I loved something, and then lost it, or it was killed . . . one of the tragedies . . . I know this is only probability, but I'm sure I would feel. My trouble is I wouldn't protest. (*Pause.*) I'm not too worried. Look at it soberly. Forgetting for the moment my face . . . the damage is not too extensive. The sexual urge is intact; like everyone else I eat, I sleep, my fingernails grow. The framework is still sound. If it comes to the worst I could always get a job in the Civil Service. The worst that can happen to me is that I'll be forgotten a bit before my time.

MILLY. You still believe that.

DON. If I were to sit down somewhere, unseen, and was quiet for a very long time, and the instinct to return to the herd petered out. All you need is four walls, and a lid.

MILLY. (*Looking around.*) In here?

DON. It's a likely spot. It's got the feel.

MILLY. But there's a street outside there, Don! All the people! Rush hour traffic. Right outside that front door!

DON. Yes. But you've got to open it, Milly. (*Pause.*) Did you, today?

MILLY. (*Suddenly conscious of herself and her predicament.*) I'm still in my nightie. I haven't got dressed . . . yet.

DON. Exactly.

MILLY. You mean . . . it can happen like this? In a dressing gown?

DON. More ways than one. (*Pause.*)

MILLY. There must be something we can do! Make a noise! . . . lest they forget, as the monument says. I can still do that. I'll make it loud, make them stop in the street, make them say: People are living there! I'll remind them. Tomorrow. (*Looking at the ceiling.*) And he's gone to sleep. It's always easier when he's asleep, even when I was up there with him. I think calmly. Quite honestly, I saw it coming. I still hate him of course. (*Takes out another cigarette.*) Sit out this last fag with me and then you can go.

DON. Promise?

MILLY. Promise, It's hell, isn't it. Open your mouth and it starts again . . . the old song and dance. (DON *is tearing off the backs of the cigarette boxes on which he made his notes during the course of the night.* MILLY *watches him.*) What's the score for tonight.

DON. (*Looking at his notes.*) On paper it looks like a draw. But I stopped halfway. It's a pity. You came out with some good things towards the end.

MILLY. I was on form.

DON. (*Examing his notes.*) Your secret? You and Ahlers?

MILLY. Meant to be. I suppose it's more of a mystery, really. Life.

DON. With a capital F. Remember that? I thought it was rather good.

MILLY. What else?

DON. Let's see. Yes . . . you said you would rather do away with yourself than carry on like this.

MILLY. Did I really?

DON. And quick. The simplest method of course is the brown paper bag. Just put it on and breathe.

MILLY. The old plunge. Head first.

DON. It's supposed to be painless. (*Looks at his notes again.*) Shorty said he'd love Sissy even if she only had one leg and one eye.

MILLY. That's big of him. She'd have to hop wouldn't she. (*Small chuckle.*) I don't mean to be cruel, Don, but when it comes to sights and sore eyes! My God, you could do something with the lot of us in here if you had a sense of humour. Can you see it? You with your head in a brown paper bag, telling the world it's painless. Sissy jumping around on one leg like a whatsis-name . . . that thing with a pouch.

DON. Kangaroo.

MILLY. Chasing Shorty! And him wiping away his tears with his boxing gloves on.

DON. And you in the middle of the mess.

MILLY. As per usual!

DON. Trying not to laugh!

MILLY. Why?

DON. Because we've all got blue bums.

(MILLY's *amusement breaks into laughter. Repeating random images from the picture just drawn— kangaroo, boxing gloves, blue bums, etc., etc.,— her laughter grows enormous. At its height, and with* DON *watching her . . .)*

CURTAIN

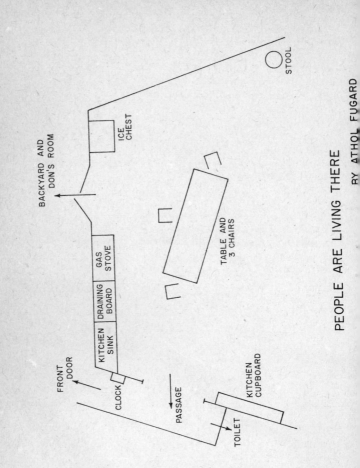

PEOPLE ARE LIVING THERE

BY ATHOL FUGARD

VERONICA'S ROOM

IRA LEVIN

(Little Theatre) Mystery

2 Men, 2 Women, Interior

VERONICA'S ROOM is, in the words of one reviewer, "a chew-up-your-finger-nails thriller-chiller" in which "reality and fantasy are entwined in a totally absorbing spider web of who's-doing-what-to-whom." The heroine of the play is 20-year-old Susan Kerner, a Boston University student who, while dining in a restaurant with Larry Eastwood, a young lawyer, is accosted by a charming elderly Irish couple, Maureen and John Mackey (played on Broadway by Eileen Heckart and Arthur Kennedy). These two are overwhelmed by Susan's almost identical resemblance to Veronica Brabissant, a long-dead daughter of the family for whom they work. Susan and Larry accompany the Mackeys to the Brabissant mansion to see a picture of Veronica, and there, in Veronica's room, which has been preserved as a shrine to her memory, Susan is induced to impersonate Veronica for a few minutes in order to solace the only surviving Brabissant, Veronica's addled sister who lives in the past and believes that Veronica is alive and angry with her. "Just say you're not angry with her," Mrs. Mackey instructs Susan. "It'll be such a blessin' for her!" But once Susan is dressed in Veronica's clothes, and Larry has been escorted downstairs by the Mackeys, Susan finds herself locked in the room and locked in the role of Veronica. Or is she really Veronica, in the year 1935, pretending to be an imaginary Susan?

The play's twists and turns are, in the words of another critic, "like finding yourself trapped in someone else's nightmare," and "the climax is as jarring as it is surprising." "Neat and elegant thriller."—*Village Voice.*

ROYALTY, $50–$35

MY FAT FRIEND

CHARLES LAURENCE

(Little Theatre) Comedy

3 Men, 1 Woman, Interior

Vicky, who runs a bookshop in Hampstead, is a heavyweight. Inevitably she suffers, good-humouredly enough, the slings and arrows of the two characters who share the flat over the shop; a somewhat glum Scottish youth who works in an au pair capacity, and her lodger, a not-so-young homosexual. When a customer—a handsome bronzed man of thirty—seems attracted to her she resolves she will slim by hook or by crook. Aided by her two friends, hard exercise, diet and a graph, she manages to reduce to a stream-lined version of her former self—only to find that it was her rotundity that attracted the handsome book-buyer in the first place. When, on his return, he finds himself confronted by a sylph his disappointment is only too apparent. The newly slim Vicky is left alone once more, to be consoled (up to a point) by her effeminate lodger.

"My fat Friend is abundant with laughs."—*Times Newsmagazine.* "If you want to laugh go."—*WCBS-TV.*

ROYALTY, $50–$35

PROMENADE, ALL!
DAVID V. ROBISON

(Little Theatre) Comedy
3 Men, 1 Woman, Interior

Four actors play four successive generations of the same family, as their business grows from manufacturing buttons to a conglomerate of international proportions (in the U.S. their perfume will be called Belle Nuit; but in Paris, Enchanted Evening). The Broadway cast included Richard Backus, Anne Jackson, Eli Wallach and Hume Cronyn. Miss Jackson performed as either mother or grandmother, as called for; and Cronyn and Wallach alternated as fathers and grandfathers; with Backus playing all the roles of youth. There are some excellent cameos to perform, such as the puritanical mother reading the Bible to her son without realizing the sexual innuendoes; or the 90-year-old patriarch who is agreeable to trying an experiment in sexology but is afraid of a heart attack.

"So likeable; jolly and splendidly performed."—N.Y. *Daily News*. "The author has the ability to write amusing lines, and there are many of them."—*N.Y. Post*. "Gives strong, lively actors a chance for some healthy exercise. And what a time they have at it!"—*CBS-TV*.

ROYALTY, $50–$35

ACCOMMODATIONS
NICK HALL

(Little Theatre) Comedy
2 Men, 2 Women, Interior

Lee Schallert, housewife, feeling she may be missing out on something, leaves her husband, Bob, and her suburban home and moves into a two-room Greenwich Village apartment with two roommates. One roommate, Pat, is an aspiring actress, never out of characters or costumes, but, through an agency mix up, the other roommate is a serious, young, graduate student—male. The ensuing complications make a hysterical evening.

"An amusing study of marital and human relations . . . a gem . . . It ranks as one of the funniest ever staged."—*Labor Herald*. "The audience at Limestone Valley Dinner Theater laughed at "Accommodations" until it hurt."—*News American*. "Superior theater, frivolous, perhaps, but nonetheless superior. It is light comedy at its best."—*The Sun, Baltimore*.

ROYALTY, $50–25

THE GOOD DOCTOR
NEIL SIMON

(All Groups) Comedy

2 Men, 3 Women. Various settings.

With Christopher Plummer in the role of the Writer, we are introduced to a composite of Neil Simon and Anton Chekhov, from whose short stories Simon adapted the capital vignettes of this collection. Frances Sternhagen played, among other parts, that of a harridan who storms a bank and upbraids the manager for his gout and lack of money. A father takes his son to a house where he will be initiated into the mysteries of sex, only to relent at the last moment, and leave the boy more perplexed than ever. In another sketch a crafty seducer goes to work on a wedded woman, only to realize that the woman has been in command from the first overture. Let us not forget the classic tale of a man who offers to drown himself for three rubles. The stories are droll, the portraits affectionate, the humor infectious, and the fun unending.

"As smoothly polished a piece of work as we're likely to see all season."—*N.Y. Daily News.* "A great deal of warmth and humor —vaudevillian humor—in his retelling of these Chekhovian tales."—*Newhouse Newspapers.* "There is much fun here . . . Mr. Simon's comic fancy is admirable."—*N.Y. Times.*

$1.75 (Music available. Write for particulars.)
ROYALTY, $50–$35

The Prisoner of Second Avenue
NEIL SIMON

(All Groups) Comedy

2 Men, 4 Women, Interior

Mel is a well-paid executive of a fancy New York company which has suddenly hit the skids and started to pare the payroll. Anxiety doesn't help; Mel, too, gets the ax. His wife takes a job to tide them over, then she too is sacked. As if this weren't enough, Mel is fighting a losing battle with the very environs of life. Polluted air is killing everything that grows on his terrace; the walls of the high-rise apartment are paper-thin, so that the private lives of a pair of German stewardesses next door are open books to him; the apartment is burgled; and his psychiatrist dies with $23,000 of his money. Mel does the only thing left for him to do: he has a nervous breakdown. It is on recovery that we come to esteem him all the more. For Mel and his wife and people like them have the resilience, the grit to survive.

"Now all this, mind you, is presented primarily in humorous terms."—*N.Y. Daily News.* "A gift for taking a grave subject and, without losing sight of its basic seriousness, treating it with hearty but sympathetic humor . . . A talent for writing a wonderfully funny line . . . full of humor and intelligence . . . Fine fun."—*N.Y. Post.* "Creates an atmosphere of casual cataclysm, and everyday urban purgatory of copelessness from which laughter seems to be released like vapor from the city's manholes."—*Time.*

$1.75. ROYALTY, $50–$35

HOME-BUILT

Lighting Equipment

for The Small Stage
By THEODORE FUCHS

This volume presents a series of fourteen simplified designs for building various types of stage lighting and control equipment, with but one purpose in mind—to enable the amateur producer to acquire a complete set of stage lighting equipment at the lowest possible cost. The volume is 8½″ x 11″ in size, with heavy paper and spiral binding—features which make the volume well suited to practical workshop use.

$3.50

Community Theatre

A MANUAL FOR SUCCESS
By JOHN WRAY YOUNG

The ideal text for anyone interested in participating in Community Theatre as a vocation or avocation. "Organizing a Community Theatre," "A Flight Plan for the Early Years," "Programming for People—Not Computers," and other chapters are blueprints for solid growth. "Technical, Business and Legal Procedures" cuts a safe and solvent path through some tricky undergrowth. Essential to the library of all community theatres, and to the schools who will supply them with talent in the years to come.

$3.00